THE
TEN DAY
EDIT

THE TEN DAY
NOVELIST
BOOK THREE

THE TEN DAY EDIT

A WRITER'S GUIDE TO EDITING A NOVEL IN TEN DAYS

LEWIS JORSTAD

THE
NOVEL
SMITHY

Published by The Novel Smithy, LLC.

Printed in the United States of America.

1st Edition, 2020

ISBN (print): 978-1-7332079-4-2

ISBN (digital): 978-1-7332079-5-9

ISBN (hardcover): 978-1-7332079-8-0

https://thenovelsmithy.com/

❀ Created with Vellum

ALSO BY LEWIS JORSTAD

"It is perfectly ok to write garbage—as long as you edit brilliantly."

C. J. CHERRYH, AMERICAN AUTHOR

CONTENTS

Before you go... **How well do you really know your hero?**

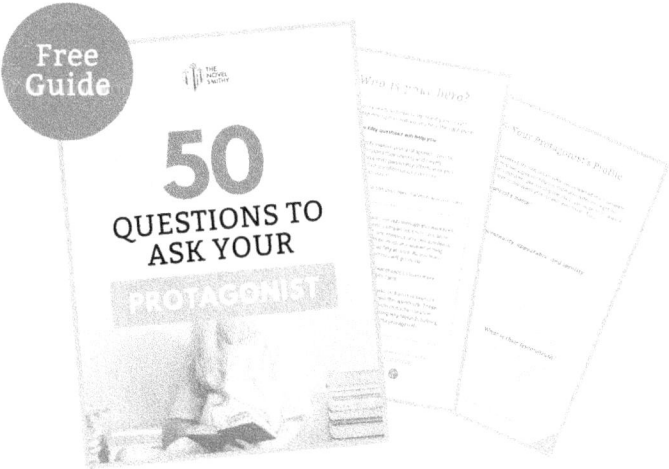

If you're ready to craft a vibrant, engaging protagonist, download your **FREE copy of 50 Questions to Ask Your Protagonist.**

This in-depth questionnaire is the perfect companion to this book, and the perfect way to get to know your hero!

https://thenovelsmithy.com/50-questions/

INTRODUCTION
LEARNING TO SWIM

Imagine yourself facing down a huge, dark wave.

You watch the water rushing towards you, and for just a moment you can hear the shouts of people coming from the beach. In an instant, the roaring wave blots out all other sounds, and even the cloudy sky on the horizon is wiped away by the looming mass of water. You can smell salt. Your eyes sting—what have you gotten yourself into?

This is what it feels like to edit a novel.

As writers, we all understand that editing is important, and that properly editing our work can be the difference between our failure or success as an author. Agents won't pay a passing glance to unedited manuscripts, and readers will quickly put down a novel that shows a lack of polish.

Still, when you sit down to face this all-important process, you'll soon realize the immense magnitude of what you're dealing with.

A novel is no small beast, and whenever you fix one problem, you'll soon realize you've created two more—like a knight struggling to slay the Hydra. You'll flip through your draft and maybe even tinker with a few scenes, but eventually, keeping your head above water will consume most of your time. It's this feeling of overwhelm that dooms so many first drafts to a desk drawer, never to see the light of day again. Even though these writers overcame the task of writing a first draft, the follow-up blow of having to edit it proved too much.

In all likelihood, you're feeling this same sense of overwhelm.

Perhaps you've pulled out your first draft after a few months away, or maybe you only just finished it yesterday. Either way, now that you've had a chance to look through this massive collection of words and characters, you've started to feel that overwhelm prickling at the back of your mind. It's hard to imagine how you could possibly bring this story together, especially when you begin to recognize the many problems lurking beneath the surface.

However, that isn't the end of your story.

You see, that mass of water looming over you might cause you nothing but dread, but a surfer would get a thrill of anticipation from that same wave. Just like they learned to love the water, you can learn to love editing too!

Weird as it may sound, I'm actually one of those people that prefers editing to writing. For me, editing is this wonderful opportunity to pull back and see the big picture of my novels. Instead of feeling pressured to get it perfect right away, I can slowly tinker with each individual piece until it all comes together as a finished story. It's truly exciting to take the rough framework I created in my first draft and sand down the rough edges until it feels complete.

Of course, no matter how much *I* might enjoy editing, that doesn't mean it doesn't come with its own unique challenges.

That feeling of overwhelm, of being swept away by the surf, is a reality even for those that thrive on the editing process. Editing a novel is a massive undertaking, and keeping yourself organized and focused is perhaps the most important thing you can do. Unfortunately, it's hard to concentrate on the task at hand when you aren't quite sure what that task is—and that's where this book comes in.

The Ten Day Edit is here to help you stay afloat, guiding you through the editing process step-by-step. Instead of struggling to edit your novel all in one go, you'll start by understanding what your story is to begin with—what is your conflict, who are your characters, and what is the real core of this adventure? From there, you can tackle the bigger picture, smoothing out the wrinkles in your plot, fleshing out your cast, and ensuring your story follows its own rules. Only once you have this solid foundation will you be ready to focus on the smaller aspects of your story, ironing out problematic scenes, creating chapters, and polishing your prose and grammar.

This is the real key to a successful edit—you can't face your novel all at once.

To that end, this book is divided into a series of chapters, each one covering one day along this ten day challenge. As you go, you'll find a set of goals at the end of each chapter, giving you an easy way to measure your progress and stay focused along the way.

However, there is a catch. If you're familiar with the previous two books in this series, you'll notice that this one works a bit differently. *The Ten Day Outline* and *The Ten Day Draft* both had easily measurable goals, whether that was scenes outlined or words written. Editing, on the other hand, is more nebulous. The time it takes to polish *your* novel may be very different from how long it takes me or any other writer to reach that same goal, because our first drafts could be in wildly different states. The process will be the same, but the amount of rewriting needed may not be.

Because of that, this book adds a few periods of rest into the mix, giving you the space to adjust the challenge to the unique needs of your first draft. This way, you won't feel like you've failed by giving your novel the time it deserves, while still knowing that you're making steady progress.

At the end of the day, all of this serves a single goal—to help you manage the overwhelming task of editing a novel, one step at a time. While that initial realization of just how much work lies ahead of you can feel like a wave threatening to pull you under, I promise you can learn to stay on top of it. Perhaps you'll even come to enjoy the ride!

So, if you're ready to take your novel to the next level, read on. I'll see you at the end of the journey.

YOUR QUESTIONS

How should I use this book?

This book is designed as a step-by-step guide, meaning each day of the challenge will build off the goals of the previous day. Fortunately, that also means each chapter will follow a similar format, so they should be easy to reference as you go through the editing process.

It's also important to note that this book will work a bit differently from either of its predecessors, *The Ten Day Outline* or *The Ten Day Draft*. Because the amount of editing your draft requires could vary dramatically, this book will focus on hunting down the flaws in your story and developing a structured game plan to fix them. The challenge will then periodically pause for you to put this plan into action, before continuing on to the next day.

If that seems confusing, don't worry—it'll make more sense when you see your game plan in action, and each chapter will feature specific goals to ensure you always know what's coming next.

How much time will I need to dedicate to this challenge?

This question is impossible to answer, for a few reasons:

- What condition is your draft in now?
- How quickly do you write on average?
- Do you already have connections with critique partners, beta readers, or editors?
- Are there any major, story-breaking flaws you'll need to address?

I've structured this challenge so that you'll spend a few days at a time identifying the problems with your story and developing a game plan to fix them. Then the challenge will pause, giving you a chance to put that plan into action at your own pace. If you don't have a ton of edits to complete, you may not need to take advantage of this pause at all—on the other hand, you may need multiple days to handle more extensive rewrites.

Ultimately, how long this challenge takes will really depend on the current state of your draft, but we'll go over how to make the most of your editing time whenever these pauses do come up. Either way, you can count on at least ten days to complete the goals set out in each chapter.

Do I have to finish this challenge in ten consecutive days?

No—in fact, you won't be able to.

Periodically, you'll find rest days built into this challenge. These are designed to give your mind a break so you can stay alert and objective when editing your story, as well as gather reader feedback and complete any necessary editing. Don't worry though—whenever we reach one of these rests, we'll go over how to maximize your time to ensure you're still making consistent progress even though the challenge is paused.

Will this be difficult?

Let me answer your question with another question—did you manage to write your first draft?

While editing comes with many of its own struggles, writing a first draft is perhaps the hardest part of finishing a novel. After all, you essentially created a whole world out of nothing! So yes, this challenge will be difficult, but no more difficult than anything else you've already accomplished. Plus, I'll be here to guide you every step of the way.

Do I need a finished first draft?

Speaking of first drafts, don't begin this challenge until you have one finished. If you're struggling to complete your first draft, check out *The Ten Day Draft* for more guidance on how to do so.

What if I've already started editing?

No problem!

If you've already begun editing your novel, I encourage you to start at the beginning of this challenge anyway. That'll ensure you take care of any problems you may have missed, while letting you breeze through the rest of the goals you've already completed.

What if I'm writing a series?

If you're writing a series, you can still use this book to guide you while you edit each draft. It'll work the same regardless of whether you edit each novel as you write them, or wait to finish the entire series before diving into editing.

Will I need to edit my novel any differently if I plan to pitch it to traditional publishers?

No, you'll go through this process exactly the same as if you were self-publishing.

Before submitting your novel to literary agents, you'll want to make sure it's in as close to its final form as possible, or else you risk unnecessary rejection letters. Unfortunately, agents simply don't have time for unedited manuscripts or stories that still need a lot of work. Your best bet at securing an agent—and a publishing deal—will require a thoroughly polished novel, the same as if you were self-publishing.

Is there anything I need to know before I start?

This book will deal with quite a few important storytelling concepts, from character development and story structure, to pacing and point of view.

While it would certainly be helpful for you to have some familiarity with these topics, I'll also make a point to explain them whenever necessary. This means you can dive into this challenge without having an in-depth knowledge of these more technical aspects of storytelling.

However, we will definitely be getting into some complex subjects, and anything you're already comfortable with will make your learning curve that much smoother. If you'd like to prepare for this challenge by reading up on some of these topics, I've created a handful of free resources and articles covering story structure and character creation that you can check out over on my website:

https://thenovelsmithy.com/

Additionally, I'll also be referencing four popular movies as examples throughout this book. While you don't have to have watched them to understand these examples, they're all excellent in their own right and well worth your time! These are:

- *Star Wars: A New Hope* (1977)
- *Princess Mononoke* (1997)
- *Mulan* (1998)
- *How to Train Your Dragon* (2010)

Will I need anything else before I start this challenge?

You're probably aware by now that this is the third book in The Ten Day Novelist series. However, you don't need to have read the previous two books to jump into this one—I'll be guiding you through everything you need, regardless of whether you've read either *The Ten Day Outline* or *The Ten Day Draft*.

Of course, that doesn't mean those two books won't be valuable to you. If you've read and followed along with either of them, certain aspects of this challenge will go by a lot more quickly. This is especially true when we create your reverse outline early on—if you've previously read *The Ten Day Outline,* you'll have already completed most of that work.

Still, if you've never cracked the front cover of those two books, don't worry! You'll be just fine going through *The Ten Day Edit* as a standalone experience.

1

DAY ZERO: WHERE TO BEGIN

There's a common misconception that writing a novel and editing one is the same thing. In reality, writing and editing couldn't be farther apart.

You see, writing is all about letting your creative brain run free. You're encouraged to wander along tangents, to explore all the places your novel could go, and to dream up wild and wonderful things to fill your story with.

Editing, on the other hand, is more analytical. As we go through the first few days of this challenge, you may be surprised to find that the bulk of your work is more about analyzing and organizing your first draft, rather than rewriting it. There will be times when you need to tap into your creativity, but for the most part, editing is about polishing what you already have through logic, reason, and structure. You've created a wild beast, and now you need to tame it.

Of course, as you can imagine, this analytical process will present its own unique challenges.

You've already managed to write a first draft, so you probably have a pretty good grip on staying productive in the face of such a huge project. Editing, however, tasks you with staying organized on top of being productive—while also accepting the flaws you find in your story along the way. At this point in the challenge, your draft will have a lot of room for improvement, but that's ok. There would be no point in editing if your novel was already perfect, after all!

So, while it may technically be cheating to have a "Day Zero" in a ten-day challenge, today will be about setting the groundwork for the rest of this editing process. Not only will you need to prepare your manuscript, but you'll also have to get yourself in the right mindset for everything to come.

From staying objective to understanding the different stages of editing, we have a lot to cover today, so let's get started.

The Need to Be Objective

Out of everything you'll face throughout this challenge, remaining an objective observer will likely be the hardest. Think about it: you've just spent anywhere from weeks to months or even years working on your first draft, bringing a story to life out of nothing. Your novel is a part of you, and staring its flaws in the face is bound to be a painful process.

Unfortunately, it's also a necessary one.

Over the next few days, you'll go through everything from minor edits to rewrites of entire scenes or characters, and it won't all be easy. Yet, perhaps the worst thing you can do— both for your novel and yourself—is kick the can down the road by avoiding the problems in your story. Far from getting rid of them, this only compounds these flaws and prolongs the editing process.

While I don't want to scare you away from this challenge, I do want to prepare you—you'll need to be ruthless to truly do your novel justice, and the key to this ruthlessness is remaining as objective as possible. There will always be a certain level of emotional attachment to your story, and that's ok—this novel is your creation, after all. Still, by and large, you'll want to think more like an outside observer of your story. This will help you recognize its flaws more willingly and handle the task of fixing them without as much internal resistance.

Of course, you know your story best, and you know what about it is most important. There's no need to abandon that core idea, but accepting when smaller elements are impeding your vision can still be hard. Unfortunately, there's no easy way to gain this objectivity. This is an internal battle you'll have to fight, but there are some things I've found helpful over the years.

For starters, keep a copy of your first draft in its raw form, separate from the one you plan to edit. This way, you'll always be able to revert back to that original draft if you want to, helping mitigate the anxiety that can come from changing aspects of your story.

From there, you'll need to take some time away.

It can be tempting to finish your first draft and then immediately jump into editing, and if you've already done so, that's ok. However, before we continue, I want you to give yourself a break. Put your story away and leave it there for at least two weeks, if not a full month.

This will not only give you the time to rest and recover from writing your first draft, but it will also help you gain a better perspective. Instead of feeling intimately tied to every aspect of your story, you'll be able to see things in a new light when you return. As a warning, be prepared—you might not like everything you find, but that's ok. That's what this editing challenge is for.

So, before we go any further, make sure you've taken at least two weeks off from your story. If you've already had a break, feel free to continue, but if not, set a reminder on your calendar to return to this book later. Set it aside with your manuscript and, once two weeks have passed, you can pick back up where you left off.

Preparing Your Manuscript

Once you're fully rested and ready to begin the editing process, you'll need to start by preparing your first draft. We'll be doing a lot of work in this document over the next few weeks, and having everything in an easy to read, easy to edit format will be a huge relief going forward.

Starting off, you'll want to standardize your manuscript into something consistent and organized—if it isn't already. To do this, make sure everything is in one place, preferably in a single file or notebook. If you wrote your draft in multiple locations, take some time to bring it all together into one cohesive document, making sure everything stays in the correct order. As you go, get rid of any chapter breaks as well —we'll be tackling chapters down the road, and you don't want them to muddy the water at this stage. For now, the only breaks in your manuscript should be for scenes or acts. Otherwise, keep your draft in a single large document.

If you wrote your draft on paper, that's about all you'll have to worry about at this stage. Shifting things over to a binder may be necessary if you wrote across multiple notebooks, but otherwise your format is pretty much set in stone. On the other hand, for those of you who wrote your first draft digitally, there are a few extra things to consider.

First off, you'll want to add page numbers to your draft—this will make it significantly easier to reference specific sections and notes later on. Most word processors will do this automatically, so experiment with yours until you find the right setting. You'll also want your entire manuscript to have a consistent font and line spacing. This is largely up to personal preference, so pick the format that will be the easiest on your eyes for long reading sessions. Additionally, if you plan to print your manuscript out and edit it physically, get a nice strong binder to keep it in. You might also consider double spacing it to give yourself room for notes and highlighting—again, anything you can do to save your eyes will be much appreciated by your future self!

Speaking of highlighting, you'll also want to create a key for your edits now, regardless of whether you'll be editing digitally or physically. This will save you from accidentally mixing up your notes later or running out of colors to use. I can't tell you how many times I've accidentally used all my color options, only to desperately need more when I start scene mapping—a topic we'll cover in a few days.

To save yourself *that* headache, make sure you decide which colors and writing utensils you'll use for these five things:

- General Notes
- Plot Points
- Scenes
- Chapter Breaks
- Mapping

For mapping specifically, you'll want to include a handful of colors you don't plan to use anywhere else, making this the perfect place for colored pencils, markers, or highlighters to come into play. To give you an example of how this could work, here's one possible setup:

- **General Notes:** Red Pen
- **Plot Points:** Blue Pen
- **Scenes:** Green Pen
- **Chapters:** Black Pen
- **Mapping:** Red, blue, yellow, orange, pink, and green highlighters, plus extra colored pencils if needed

Of course, not everyone writes in the same medium, and your first draft could be in any number of places—from a digital file, to a large binder on your desk. If pens and pencils aren't an option for you, then colored fonts, comments, and a track changes feature are worthy alternatives.

While I personally lean towards editing and writing digitally, and will likely reference digital forms often throughout this book, anything I mention will apply equally to those of you who are working on paper. The most important thing is that you're comfortable and proficient with your writing method of choice and that it allows you to organize your draft effectively—meaning now probably isn't the time to learn that fancy new writing software you haven't tried yet. Instead, stick with what you're used to, at least for this challenge.

Finding Your Editing Space

Alongside preparing your manuscript for editing, you'll also want to figure out *where* you'll edit your draft.

At first glance, this may seem like a weird requirement, especially if you're following along from either of the other books in this series. You're bound to have found some kind of writing space when working on your first draft, so why not just use that? Well, while many of the requirements for a good writing and editing space are the same, there are some differences.

For instance, writing is often best done in a space that nurtures your creativity, meaning fewer distractions and outside stimuli. Many writers even go so far as to write in complete silence because of this. On the other hand, editing is more analytical, and even if you normally write alone you may find it really helpful to edit around other people. That way, when your brain starts to fry, you can get up, walk around, talk for a bit, or even just tune into other people's sounds and conversations. Your brain stays active, but you get a chance to rest at the same time.

At the end of the day, your editing space will be personal to you and your needs, and it's entirely possible you'll prefer to edit in the same space you wrote in. Personally, I write and edit everything from my kitchen table, start to finish, but I do change how I use the space depending on what I'm working on. When writing, I work in silence, whereas I like to edit with music or videos playing in the background. Regardless of where *you* edit your novel, make sure it fulfills these things:

———

Comfort:

After a long day of editing, you don't want to throw back problems into the mix. Pick an editing space that encourages good posture and try to choose somewhere where you can get up to stretch and walk around periodically. Keeping yourself in good shape not only helps you avoid the aches and pains that come from sitting at a desk all day, but it also keeps your mind fresh.

Supplies:

You'll inevitably need some supplies while you edit. For those of you editing on paper, this might mean pens, pencils, highlighters, and a binder or notebook. On the other hand, if you're editing on your computer, make sure you have any chargers you'll need and consider keeping some scratch paper on hand for random notes. You may also choose to do some of your editing on a Kindle or tablet—more on that tomorrow. Whatever your setup looks like, your editing space should have all the supplies you need on hand, so you'll never have to interrupt your editing to go hunt down your laptop charger.

Focus:

What "focus" means while writing versus while editing could be a bit different from what you expect. Like I mentioned previously, I need complete silence to write, whereas music is no problem while editing—I'm particularly fond of the ambient nature sounds of the Animal Crossing soundtrack these days.

Understanding out your own preferences will likely take some experimenting on your part, so take a moment to think about what kind of space will be most conducive to your ability to focus. Whether or not you work well in noisier places, try to find a space where you won't be regularly interrupted by other people or things, while still giving you plenty of outlets for when you start to feel burnt out.

Purpose:

As you might imagine, few coffee shops or libraries are specifically dedicated to "editing," meaning your editing space's purpose is more of a mental distinction.

Don't edit in bed, on your couch, or anywhere that your brain strongly associates with relaxation, procrastination, or rest. If you have a home office already dedicated to work, that's great, but a co-working space, library, or even your dining room table is fine too. Regardless of where you work, develop a mental separation that'll clue your brain in to when it's time for work-mode rather than rest-mode.

———

No matter where you end up editing your novel, if you ever find yourself struggling with your writing space, come back to this section and reevaluate it—often, a simple change in atmosphere is all you need to get your head back into the right place.

The Four Stages of Editing

If you're following along from the previous two books in this series, then you'll quickly notice some key differences. In those books, I had you set specific goals from the very start of the challenge and create a calendar with deadlines designed to keep you accountable. However, when it comes to editing your novel, that's a lot harder to do.

You see, as I mentioned earlier, outlining a novel and writing one both require roughly the same amount of work, regardless of the story being created. There's a clear end goal to work towards and a clear path to reach it. This is still true of editing to some extent, but the amount of work needed along the way can vary wildly depending on the current state of your first draft.

In an ideal world, you'll find that your draft doesn't have many major flaws to deal with, meaning your edits should go by fairly quickly. Still, it's just as possible that you'll find deeply rooted problems in your story's structure, pacing, or cast, all of which will require intense rewrites to correct. You don't want to avoid these issues, no matter how difficult they may be—buckling down and fixing them when they come up will ultimately leave you with less work to do in the long run. However, this does mean your editing experience may take a lot longer than another writer's. It really just depends.

Because of this, you won't be creating any hard deadlines at this stage. You see, while this book *is* about editing your novel in the broad sense, what that means in practice is a few different things. Editing can encompass anything from a complete rewrite of your plot to simply correcting a few typos, and everything in between. Specifically, this challenge will split the editing process into four distinct stages:

———

Big-Picture Editing:

These edits will focus on the building blocks of your novel—your plot, story structure, characters, and conflict.

This is when you'll look at whether your story is delivering on its promises and working as a whole, along with making sure there aren't any gaping holes or story-breaking problems to address. You'll want to get these fixes out of the way before doing anything else, or risk having to redo a lot of work later on.

Mid-Level Editing:

Mid-level editing is where you'll get to dig into the smaller units of your story—your scenes and chapters. Things like scene structure, pacing, and chapter structure will all come into play here. Essentially, this is where you polish the moment-by-moment beats of your story, turning it into a compelling page-turner for your readers.

Gathering Feedback:

Feedback is an essential part of editing a novel, regardless of whether or not you work with a professional editor. We'll be going over a few places to look for feedback, as well as how to process the feedback you receive. This will give you a chance to get a second set of eyes on your story and to catch any big-picture or mid-level flaws you may have missed.

Prose and Proofreading:

Once all the above stages are complete, you can get into the nitty-gritty wordsmithing of your novel. Here you'll tweak your descriptions, dialog, word choice, rhythm, and tone, as well as check your manuscript for typos and inconsistencies. Last but not least, you'll nail down your opening line and choose a final title for your novel!

————

While we'll definitely be setting concrete goals down the road, we won't worry about them just yet. Instead, we'll tackle each of these sections in their own unique ways, allowing you to give your manuscript the attention it needs regardless of how much editing your first draft requires.

By setting goals at different stages of this journey, you'll also be able to more accurately estimate what needs to get done and when, meaning your editing challenge should go much more smoothly overall.

The Goals of Day Zero

With all your preparation complete, you're officially ready to wrap up Day Zero. Though you didn't get any editing done today, you did lay the groundwork that will make the rest of this editing process that much easier.

Of course, while preparing your manuscript and choosing an editing space is important, by far the most important part of today's goals is getting into the right mindset. Taking a step back from your manuscript and learning to be objective about your story will serve you well in the coming days. If you take nothing else away from today, remember that every change you make throughout this challenge will be in the service of strengthening your final novel—even if it isn't easy in the moment.

Tomorrow we'll begin reviewing your manuscript, but for now, here are the goals you've completed for Day Zero:

1. Spend a minimum of two weeks away from your novel to get a more objective look at your story.
2. Compile your draft in one organized place, such as a single document or binder.
3. Create a color-coded key for the different types of editing you'll be doing.
4. Choose an editing space and set it up with any necessary supplies.

On to Day One!

2

DAY ONE: THE JOURNEY BACK

Every adventure is bound to have a few snags along the way. Whether you get a flat tire in the middle of an endless desert, wake up an angry dragon in a distant land, or simply miss your connecting flight, these setbacks are all part of the journey. When you're back home safe and sound, they'll make good stories to share around the dinner table, and for the most part you'll forget the stress you felt in that moment. It's easy to laugh about being lost and afraid when you're sitting safely back on your own couch, after all.

In many ways, writing your first draft follows this same pattern. You undoubtedly hit some bumps along the way— perhaps even some major ones—but now that you're holding your finished draft in your hands, it's easy to forget about those problems.

Editing changes all that.

Not only does editing force you to come face to face with the difficulties you experienced while writing your first draft, but it'll also lay bare every flaw in your story and every error you made. That rosy outlook you had when you finally finished your draft will melt away all too quickly, replaced instead with an equal mix of embarrassment and frustration.

Unfortunately, today is when you'll have to bear the brunt of these emotions, because today is when you'll read through your draft for the first time. In fact, you won't be doing much else—other than a bit of housekeeping to prepare you for Day Two, Day One is all about refamiliarizing yourself with your novel.

However, with these challenges comes a brighter side—if you can get through this first reading, you can get through any part of the editing process!

As strange as that may sound, it really is true. If you can face down the flaws in your story and keep marching ahead anyways, you've officially overcome the biggest hurdle along your editing journey. Take heart—there may be dragons ahead, but each one has its weaknesses, and each one will be defeated in due time. For now, we need to figure out what we're dealing with.

The First Reading

While it may seem silly to read through your entire draft from beginning to end—you did just finish writing it after all —this stage of the editing process is an important one, because it gives you your first big-picture look at your story.

Writing a first draft is an intense process, and it's easy to forget how your story starts by the time you write "the end." So, before you can begin editing, you'll need to refamiliarize yourself with the story you've created. What are its strengths, and what about its weaknesses? Basically, this first reading will help you get into the minds of your readers, and will make it that much easier tomorrow when we begin analyzing your story.

Of course, while reading your manuscript is fairly simple, that doesn't mean there aren't some specific things you'll want to think about today.

For starters, what is the ideal format for reading your draft?

If you wrote it on paper, you're pretty much locked into that format. However, for those of you that wrote your draft digitally, you have a few more options. You could read it in the word processor you wrote it in, but you could also print it out and put it in a binder, or even upload it to your Kindle or tablet. Whatever you choose to do, the idea is to make it as easy and comfortable for you to read as possible, while still having space to take notes when needed. In fact, I strongly encourage you to consider completing this first reading in a format other than the one you wrote in, if possible. This will help you see your words in a new light, and will keep the experience fresh. Anything you can do to keep your brain engaged is a good thing, because it'll make it that much easier for you to truly *see* your novel.

For those of you who want to transfer your draft over to a tablet, smartphone, or e-reader, there are a few ways to go about this.

Perhaps the easiest is to upload your draft to Google Docs and use the Google Drive app on your phone or tablet to read your manuscript. You could also convert your draft to a PDF and upload it to your tablet over email, though you'll need another place to take notes if you pursue this option. Finally, you could upload it to your Kindle or other e-reader. This is more difficult to achieve, but you can absolutely do it if you'd like to. Simply search "How to Put Your Novel on the

Kindle App as an E-Book File" online and follow the instructions you find. Unfortunately, they're a bit too involved for me to relay here, and the most up-to-date method changes frequently as well.

Once your draft is ready to read, you can get started. Grab a cup of coffee, a snack, or a glass of water, curl up in a comfy chair, and dive in!

As you go, make a point to correct any glaring typos or misspellings as they come up—or at least mark them when you find them. This shouldn't distract from your reading too much, and it'll make for a quicker proofreading process down the road. However, don't let yourself obsess over this. It's fine to miss errors at this stage, so just fix the ones that stand out. Likewise, jot down any thoughts or concerns that come up while you read. If a section of your story doesn't feel right, circle or underline it. If you have more detailed notes, feel free to write those down too. Basically, anything you think you might like to revisit down the road should have a small note left next to it.

Of course, there's a caveat to all this: this isn't the time to actually apply those fixes.

At this stage, all you should be doing is taking notes and correcting any small typos you find. Instead of worrying about how to fix those larger errors, simply make a record of them and move on. Like I said above, we'll get to these problems in due time—for now, your focus should just be on reading through your draft and refamiliarizing yourself with your story.

Only once you've finished reading your draft from beginning to end will you be ready to work on it.

Defining Your Story

With your first reading complete, it's time to set up the start of your reverse outline. This will be the main organizational tool you'll use throughout this challenge, and you'll be referencing it a lot. From breaking down your novel's structure to analyzing your scenes or characters, this reverse outline will be the foundation from which you complete almost all of your big-picture and mid-level editing.

Of course, some of you will be jumping into this book having previously read either *The Ten Day Outline* or *The Ten Day Draft*. If that's the case, then you should already have at least some kind of outline for your novel. So what's with all this talk of a reverse outline? If you already have an outline, does that mean you need to do it all over again?

The short answer is—no.

If you've already outlined your novel, the reverse outlining process will go much more quickly than if you were setting it up from scratch, and this is especially true if you're using the outline you created during *The Ten Day Outline*. Instead of having to build your reverse outline from the ground up, you should already have most everything in place, and will only need to update your existing outline with new details and information about your first draft.

However, that doesn't mean I'll leave you out in the cold if you have no preexisting outline to work from. Whether you already have an outline or are starting completely from scratch, we'll be going over everything your reverse outline needs over the next few days.

While we'll talk more about the many benefits and uses of a reverse outline tomorrow, the short version is that your reverse outline will act as a guide for your story. Whenever you have a question or need to record a change, you'll turn to your outline. Likewise, when you need to reference a scene or section, you'll open up your outline, rather than flipping through pages and pages of your manuscript. Essentially, your reverse outline will become the central hub for all of your editing work throughout this challenge, making it an essential tool—and something you'll want to start off right!

Fortunately, this won't take long, regardless of whether you already have an outline or not.

If you already have an outline to work from, pull it out. If not, open a new document or flip to a new page in your notebook. Keep in mind that, just because you wrote your draft on paper doesn't mean you can't reverse outline it digitally, and vice versa. Regardless of where you start your outline, make sure your medium of choice will allow you to easily create lists, take notes, and move things around if needed. A binder is great for this, as is a digital document— while a notebook with its unmovable pages is less ideal.

Whatever you choose, turn to the top of the page and write down your novel's working title, the date, and "reverse outline." If you have no idea what you want to call your novel at this stage—which is completely fine—then feel free to skip that step. Then, make a record of these five things:

- Your Premise
- Your Story's Conflict
- The Dramatic Question
- Your Point of View
- Your Story's Theme

If you already have an outline to work from, just make sure it covers these five things and that they're still an accurate reflection of your first draft. Don't be alarmed if you need to tweak them slightly either—it's natural for your draft to evolve as you write it, and aspects of your story may have changed along the way.

Of course, you may not understand what some of these mean, so here are a few quick definitions:

———

Your Premise:

Your premise is the elevator pitch of your story. This should be a one to two sentence description that includes who your main character is, what their initial goal will be, and what types of conflict they'll face. There's no need to include any specific details like event or character names here, so instead focus on summarizing your story as succinctly as possible.

Once you've created this premise, you can use it to see which parts of your story are truly impacting this core idea, and which parts are just extra.

Your Story's Conflict:

Conflict is what drives the plot and progression of your story. What are your characters fighting against, and what is forcing them to take action?

This will be the core conflict of your novel as a whole, and you should be able to summarize it in a sentence or two. Every scene in your story should tie back to this conflict in some way, ensuring your novel is cohesive and giving it a strong direction.

The Dramatic Question:

This is a summary of your story, framed as a question. For instance, "Will Frodo destroy the One Ring?" is the Dramatic Question of J. R. R. Tolkien's *The Lord of the Rings*.

Your Dramatic Question should identify who your main character is and what their primary goal will be throughout your story. How you answer this will determine the ending of your novel, and this will be the primary question your readers ask themselves throughout your story.

Your Point of View:

Point of view is the perspective from which your story is told, and you may already be familiar with its abbreviation: POV. There are four points of view commonly used in fiction, and we'll get into more detail on how each one works later in the challenge. For now, you can tell which point of view you're using based on who "tells" your story:

- **First Person POV:** The entire story is told by your protagonist, using "I did/thought/felt/saw/etc…"
- **Peripheral First Person POV:** This is the same as First Person POV, except the story's narrator is not the protagonist.
- **Limited Third Person POV:** Here the narrator is not a character in the story at all, but an outside observer who follows the experiences of a single character. The story is told using "he/she/they."
- **Omniscient Third Person POV:** This POV uses "he/she/they," but is not limited to any single character's experiences. This narrator can recount all the events and experiences of every character in the story without limit.

Your Story's Theme:

Theme is a nebulous concept, but at its core it's the unifying idea that ties your entire story together. Of course, that means it isn't always easy to identify. If you don't have a strong idea of your theme yet, that's ok—still, try your best to write down something related to theme.

Some writers think of this as their novel's moral center or the lesson it's trying to teach. Others think of theme as the core idea of their story, such as the meaning of justice, the relationship between generations, what it means to be honorable, or even something as open-ended as the different forms of power. There's no need to take a hard stance here either—this theme will simply help you ensure that everything in your story connects on a fundamental level, something we'll discuss more later on.

———

As you fill out these five things, reference your manuscript as much as you need. Alternatively, make sure your existing outline covers each of these instead.

From there, there's no need to worry about transferring the notes you took during your first reading to your reverse outline, at least for now. Once you've recorded these five things, your work for today is done!

The Goals of Day One

While this will be one of the shorter chapters in this challenge, this will also probably be one of your longer editing days, simply because you had to read your entire manuscript. You're sure to have run into some stressful things as you went, but just remember—we'll handle all of it in due time.

Instead, today was just about getting a solid grasp on the current state of your story. Tomorrow we'll begin breaking down your draft into more manageable chunks, and soon you'll have a detailed game plan to help you start the editing process. In the meantime, put your draft away and go take a much-needed rest. Today was a long day, and we have a lot more work ahead of us.

Tomorrow we'll begin analyzing the many pieces of your story, but for now, here are the goals you've completed for Day One:

1. Read your manuscript, taking notes on anything you'd like to revisit later.
2. Start your reverse outline by recording your story's premise, conflict, Dramatic Question, point of view, and theme.

On to Day Two!

3

DAY TWO: UNDERSTANDING THE STORY YOU'VE GOT

Have you ever tried to pat your head and rub your stomach at the same time? As silly as this schoolyard trick is, it's actually a great example of a problem many writers run into when editing their novels: trying to do two opposing things at once is almost always a recipe for failure.

You see, editing isn't one straightforward process—there are actually two distinct phases you'll go through when editing a novel. For starters, you'll need to analyze and process your story's strengths and weaknesses, but you'll also need to actually rewrite that story to correct the flaws you find. The first of these two phases is almost entirely logic-based, more about sorting through the many puzzle pieces of your story than anything else. Only once you understand the current state of your draft can you start putting that puzzle together, flexing your creative muscles as you dream up ways to fill in the gaps of your novel.

What this all means is that, just like trying to pat your head and rub your stomach, analyzing your story and putting that analysis into action can easily cancel each other out. It's simply too hard for your brain to flip between such different tasks in short succession and, as a result, you end up doing neither well.

So, rather than making your life harder for no good reason, we'll be putting rewrites to the side for a few days. Instead, this portion of your ten-day editing challenge will be all about creating a big-picture, holistic map of your draft, and then using that map to truly understand the story you've created. This is where that all-important reverse outline I keep mentioning will come together—but of course, that won't all happen in one day.

Today, we'll just be focusing on the larger elements of your reverse outline—your story's structure, your character sheets, and your story's rulebook. Add in the notes you took on Day One and you'll be well on your way to understanding every nook and cranny of your novel!

Starting Your Reverse Outline

By the time it's finished, your reverse outline will have essentially become a shorthand version of your novel. It'll contain all the same things, including your plot, characters, and worldbuilding, just condensed into a few pages of highly organized notes.

So, why call it a "reverse" outline? It sounds just like a normal outline, right?

Well, the reason for this name is that you'll be outlining your novel backwards. Whereas you complete a typical outline before you ever sit down to write your novel, this one will ask you to go back through your first draft and outline everything you've already written.

This serves two purposes. For starters, it gives you an easy way to see the big-picture of your story and to identify any problems it has without having to sift through your entire manuscript to find them. Second, it forces you to think about your story in a new way. By the end of this process, you'll find that you see your story in a new light, noticing things like pacing and structure far more than you ever would have otherwise.

Of course, as I mentioned yesterday, you may already have a preexisting outline to work with. If that's the case, then today should go by fairly quickly. As you complete today's goals, all you'll need to do is make sure your current outline accurately reflects the state of your first draft, adding in anything that may be missing. On the other hand, if you don't have an outline or if the one you do have is sparse, you'll need to follow along with today's goals more closely.

So, to start fleshing out your reverse outline, skip a line or two below the information you recorded yesterday. This is where we'll begin organizing your story's structure.

If you're unfamiliar with the idea of story structure, this is the basic framework within which your plot is told, and it provides some common guidelines for better understanding what a well-paced plot looks like. At their core, story structures are really just culturally recognized forms of storytelling, collectively developed over centuries to provide a loose skeleton for what a compelling story looks like— making them a useful tool for analyzing your own novel.

While there are a whole variety of structures out there, for this challenge we'll be focusing on the Three Act Structure. This is perhaps the most popular story structure found in Western storytelling, showing up in everything from Hollywood blockbusters to indie literary novels. Basically any story can fit within these guidelines, so don't worry if you're unsure whether or not your story will work within this framework. The Three Act Structure is well-known for being one of the most intuitive and flexible story structures out there, especially for those of us who grew up regularly exposed to Western films and books. You may even find you recognize some elements of this structure, even if you've never heard them called out by name!

Since the Three Act Structure will come up more and more often as we dig deeper into this challenge, let's define some basic terms you'll need to know, starting with acts:

- **Act 1 (Setup):** Act 1 comprises the first quarter of your story and is all about preparing your cast for the journey ahead. This is where you'll introduce your setting, protagonist, and the main conflict they'll be facing.
- **Act 2 (Confrontation):** Act 2 forms the bulk of your story, around 50%. All the adventures, twists, and turns happen here, giving you time to flesh out your characters, backstories, and settings. Most importantly, Act 2 contains a major turning point where your protagonist shifts from reacting to the conflict to actively trying to resolve it thanks to the new skills and knowledge they've gained thus far.
- **Act 3 (Resolution):** Act 3 is the final quarter of your novel and sees the conflict come to its end. Here your protagonist and antagonist will have their final confrontation. Once you resolve the conflict of your story, you'll have a moment to hint at the future and explain what happens after your protagonist's journey is over (or set up a sequel, if you're planning one).

When combined, these acts will form the three main units of your story, coming together to create the foundation of the Three Act Structure. Alongside these three acts, the Three Act Structure also has a total of eleven plot points, though we'll only be focusing on six for the sake of this book:

The Hook:

This is the scene that opens your story. It's designed to catch your reader's attention and encourage them to keep reading by introducing them to a unique aspect of your world or characters. It is also a promise to your reader, and sets the tone for everything to come after.

The First Plot Point:

This is the moment your story really begins, and it's also when Act 1 ends. Your protagonist has spent Act 1 learning about the conflict they're about to face, and here they'll finally become fully involved in the events of your story thanks to a pivotal decision they'll have to make.

The Midpoint:

This is the next major turning point of your story.

Your Midpoint marks the half-way point in your novel and sees your protagonist face a major challenge. By overcoming this challenge they'll gain new skills or knowledge that will allow them to start actively shaping the events of your story. From here on out, they have a plan for overcoming the conflict, even if that plan might fail later.

The Third Plot Point:

This plot point marks the end of Act 2 and is a harsh reality check for your protagonist. Here they'll suffer a major defeat at the hands of your antagonist, throwing their previous plans into disarray. This will be their lowest moment, when they feel like they've lost everything. In the following scenes, they'll need to reassess their goals in order to recommit to the journey ahead.

The Climax:

This is the final conflict between your protagonist and antagonist. It may be a major battle, a confession of love, or a heated confrontation. Whatever it is, your protagonist will need to draw on all the skills, knowledge, and alliances they've gained throughout your story if they want to succeed. Alternatively, they may fail.

The Resolution:

These are the last few scenes of your story, meant to show your readers the final effects of your Climax. Whether your protagonist succeeded or failed in their quest, here you'll take a moment to say some final goodbyes and show what your story's world now looks like. You may also be laying the groundwork for sequels here.

————

When looked at as a whole, the Three Act Structure helps you create a story with a slowly rising and falling tension as the conflict of your novel progresses. This tension spikes at the First Plot Point, Midpoint, and Climax in particular, as these should be the most significant moments of change in your story. The First Plot Point sets the action of your plot in motion, the Midpoint is the biggest turning point for your protagonist, and the Climax is where their entire journey comes to fruition.

However, this structure isn't entirely linear either, with the tension fluctuating between the various plot-points in the story. Put together, the Three Act Structure looks something like this, with the rising green line representing the increasing tension of the story as the conflict develops:

THE THREE ACT STRUCTURE

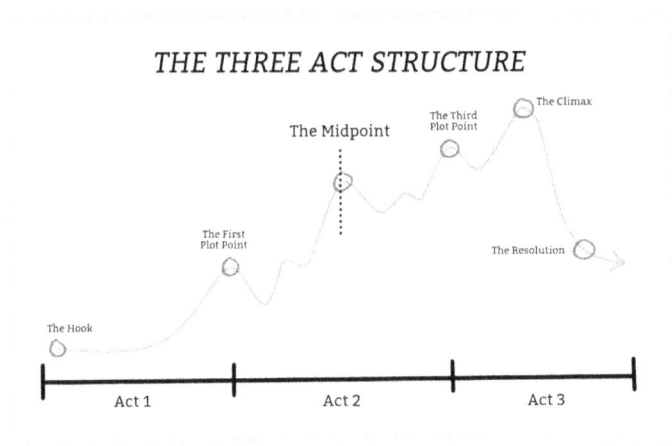

Of course, it can help to see this structure at work in a real story, so let's look at the plot of *Star Wars: A New Hope* broken down with these six plot points:

The Hook:

Darth Vader intercepts Princess Leia's ship in search of stolen plans for the Death Star. However, Princess Leia sneaks them out of his grasp with the help of R2-D2.

The First Plot Point:

Upon returning home with Obi-Wan, Luke finds that Stormtroopers have killed his aunt and uncle. Now with a personal reason to hate the Empire, Luke joins Obi-Wan, and the two set out to find Princess Leia.

The Midpoint:

While searching for Alderaan, a tractor beam pulls the Millennium Falcon aboard the Death Star. They must now escape, made even more complex when they realize Princess Leia is also on board.

The Third Plot Point:

Obi-Wan sacrifices himself in a battle with Darth Vader to buy Luke and his friends enough time to escape the Death Star. Luke is powerless as he watches Darth Vader kill his mentor.

The Climax:

As the Death Star approaches the Rebel base, Luke and the other Rebel pilots scramble to destroy it. With Han Solo's help and his own trust in the Force, Luke blows up the Death Star. Unknown to the Rebels, Darth Vader narrowly escapes.

The Resolution:

The movie ends during a large ceremony, with Princess Leia honoring Han and Luke for their role in destroying the Death Star.

————

Applying the Three Act Structure to your own story should be fairly simple, and you'll be using the exact same template I used above.

To get started, write down each of the six plot points we've just discussed:

- Hook
- First Plot Point
- Midpoint
- Third Plot Point
- Climax
- Resolution

Then, look back through your story—which scenes best match the requirements of each of these plot points?

Some of these should be fairly easy to identify, such as the Midpoint, which always falls right around the halfway point of your novel. Others like the First Plot Point, might give you more trouble, so don't be afraid to take your time identifying these if needed. Whenever you decide which scene in your story best fits each plot point, jot down a short description of what happens in that scene along with the page number it starts on. Don't worry if your story doesn't perfectly match these plot points either—that's a problem we'll tackle later in the challenge.

Finally, before you finish this portion of your reverse outline, write a short one to two paragraph summary for each of the three acts in your story. These should roughly cover any major events, which characters are involved, and what the outcome is. Remember that Act 1 spans the Hook to the First Plot Point, Act 2 spans the end of the First Plot Point to the Third Plot Point, and Act 3 spans the end of the Third Plot Point to the Resolution.

Analyzing Your Cast

With your story's structure roughly outlined, you're ready to start building a record of your novel's cast. Of course, as was the case with story structure, there will be some important technical terms and concepts you'll need to understand— we'll get to those in just a moment.

For now, start this section of your reverse outline by skipping a few lines below the work you just completed and listing every named character in your story. Beside their name, jot down a brief description of the role they play in your story, as well as their primary goal and personality. Just hit the highlights here—there's no need to go into exhaustive depth quite yet.

Of course, there will be some characters you'll want a more detailed record of, specifically your core cast.

If you're unfamiliar with this term, these are the characters that play the most active role in your story, and will therefore have the most information for you to record. This will obviously include your protagonist and antagonist, but your core cast could also include important mentor figures, allies, and enemies as well. To help you pick out which characters from your list belong in your core cast, consider these questions for each:

- Do they have a significant influence on the outcome of your conflict?
- Will they be a regular presence throughout your protagonist's journey?
- Do they oppose or challenge your protagonist and their allies in a meaningful way?

- Will readers see them grow and change significantly as the story progresses?
- Do they meaningfully impact your protagonist, either as an ally, mentor, or enemy?

You should include any character that meets one or more of these requirements in your core cast, so mark their name in the list you just created. As a rough estimate, most novels will have a core cast of anywhere from five to ten characters, though this will ultimately depend on your unique story. Fantasy and science fiction novels tend to have much larger casts in general, while a cozy romance may only have five named characters at all. At the end of the day, focus on quality over quantity here.

Once you feel confident you've marked all the characters within your core cast, you can flesh out their entries in your list into fully fledged character sheets. This will help you get a better idea of how they grow and change throughout your story, and you'll turn to these character sheets often in the coming days.

To do this, we're going to use a simple template just like we did for story structure. This will help you keep everything organized and make it easy to reference your character sheets down the road. So, for each character in your core cast, write down:

- Your character's name, alongside a short description of who they are and their relationship to any other characters.
- Your character's main goal
- A brief paragraph outlining their background or personal history
- Key terms to describe their personality

- Additional terms to describe their flaws
- Any other important information you want to record, such as physical appearance, skills, or special knowledge

Then, repeat this template for your entire cast.

If you're following along from *The Ten Day Outline*, all of this should already be present in your existing character sheets. However, in addition to this information you'll also want to record a few extra additional things unique to your reverse outline:

- Where each character is and what they're doing during each of the six plot points in your story.
- How they impact your story's conflict and plot as a whole.
- Why they uniquely matter to your story.
- What they bring to the table that another character couldn't.

These extra notes should give you a good idea of exactly how your core characters are impacting your story, and will make analyzing them much easier over the next few days.

Of course, if you're at all familiar with character creation, then you'll know we're still missing one important thing—character arcs.

Character arcs are the inner journeys your characters go on throughout your story, following them as they grow and change as a result of their adventures. Many if not all of your core characters will start out in a place of dissatisfaction, and over time their goals and experiences will force them to confront the inner struggle or flaw that's holding them back.

However, not all characters will handle this self-reflection the same way. The lucky ones will learn to move past their flaws and grow into better people by the end of their journey, while some will slowly decline until they're past the point of no return. In the end, all character arcs can be explained through these three categories:

———

Positive Arc:

This is the classic "hero" story, though it can apply equally to many types of characters.

In a positive arc, the character starts out with a deep internal flaw. Throughout the course of their arc the story's conflict punishes this flaw. They face a major challenge that leads to a turning point in their arc, moving them closer to uncovering the lesson they need to learn. Ultimately—despite setbacks along the way—they learn to embrace this new truth, overcome their flaws, and succeed against the conflict of their story.

- **Examples:** Rick Blaine, Moana, Aragorn, Han Solo, Hiccup Hiccup Horrendous Haddock III

Negative Arc:

Negative arcs follow a similar trajectory as positive arcs, with the major change being at the end.

Just like a positive arc, the character begins the story with an internal flaw and—as the story progresses—uncovers an important truth, experiencing a key turning point along the way. However, unlike a positive arc, a negative arc character rejects that truth repeatedly. By the end of the story they're more entrenched in their flaws than before, growing into a worse version of themselves and failing against the conflict of their story as a result.

- **Examples:** Anakin Skywalker, Jay Gatsby, Michael Corleone, Tyler Durden, Sansa Stark

Flat Arc:

These are the black sheep of character arcs. While positive and negative arcs are "change arcs," a flat arc character already knows the truth (or lesson) at the start of the story. Instead, their arc is about upholding the truth in the face of their story's conflict, passing their lesson to others in the process.

- **Examples:** Captain America, Katniss Everdeen, Luke Skywalker, Princess Nausicaa, Mattie Ross

---

THREE TYPES OF CHARACTER ARCS

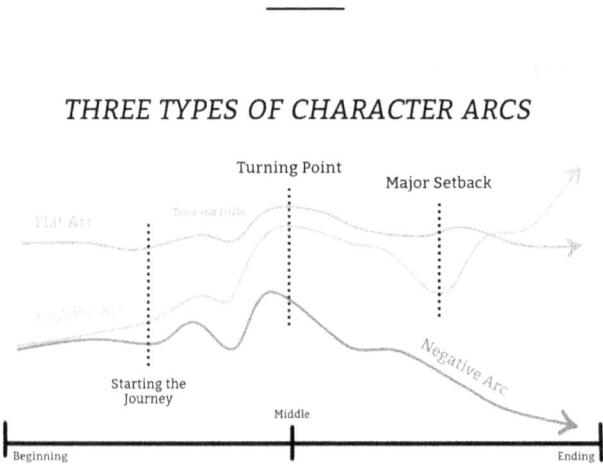

If we graph these character arcs the same way we did for the Three Act Structure, they'll end up looking something like this, with the rising or falling lines representing the character's progress towards achieving their goals and overcoming their flaws.

As I'm sure you can guess by now, character arcs are a hugely important part of writing compelling characters—however, not all characters will have them, even within your core cast.

Unfortunately, it's not always an easy task to determine which characters "should" have arcs, because so much will depend on your unique story. Your protagonist is the one exception—they will *always* have an arc of some kind, since they are the driving catalyst of your novel. Their growth and change will shape the progress of your story and will be what keeps your reader invested in the adventure, providing the emotional payoff that comes at the end of a good novel.

So, for simplicity's sake, let's start there.

Turn to your protagonist's entry in your character sheet and look over the three types of character arcs defined above. Write down where your protagonist begins—what flaw are they struggling against at the start, and what do they want to achieve? Then, flip to the very end of your novel—have they overcome this flaw, or are they in a worse place than when they began? Have they achieved their goals, and at what cost?

Your answers here will help you determine which arc your protagonist follows, and once you've figured it out, record it in their character sheet. You can then repeat this process for all of your core characters to see which ones have arcs and what types of arcs they have. For any that do have arcs, write down which type, along with their starting and ending point within that arc.

Finally, before we wrap up your character sheet, we're going to look at your character's wants and needs.

Every character with an arc will have these two elements pushing and pulling them throughout their journey, and the inner conflict caused by their want and need will drive both their motivation and their progress throughout your novel.

Your character's want is the personal desire or goal that they believe will bring fulfillment to their life, and this is what will push them to take action throughout your story. Often, this want is a manifestation of their flaw—for example, in Disney's *Mulan*, Mulan wants validation from others because she doesn't see the value in herself. Because of this flaw, she believes outside approval will fix her problems and make her happy. In reality, what she *needs* is to recognize her innate worth and value her clever and assertive personality. This need is the key to her fulfillment and to her growth within her character arc, and the same basic principle will be true for your characters as well.

So, for each character who has an arc in your novel, consider their want versus their need. At the start of their adventure, what do they believe will make them truly happy, even if it won't really? By the end, what will they need to learn in order to actually achieve happiness—whether they succeed in learning it or not?

Once you've decided these things, write down both a want and a need for every character with a character arc in your character sheet.

Your Story's Rulebook

We're finally on the home stretch of today's goals, but before we wrap things up we're going to add one more section to your reverse outline—your story's rulebook.

Just like the rules of a card game or a sport outline what's allowed and when, your story's rulebook will lay out the rules, restrictions, and history of your story's world. This will be hugely important later, though it should only take you a few minutes to record here. To create your story's rulebook, consider your entire draft and record everything you can think of based on these categories:

- Time Period
- Location
- History
- Culture
- Religion
- Social Norms or Prejudices
- Common Mannerisms
- Languages
- Technology
- Magic or Other Systems
- Flora and Fauna
- Concurrent Events

Not only will this rulebook help you keep the events of your novel consistent and believable, but it will also provide a great opportunity for you to flesh out and expand on your worldbuilding. After all, when writing your first draft you probably had a whole host of excellent ideas related to your story's world, but you may not have been able to incorporate them all effectively. Now that you can see your entire story at work, you'll be able to give your worldbuilding a boost if needed.

Of course, this will naturally be harder for some novels and easier for others.

For instance, if you're writing a contemporary romance novel, you'll only need to define things like locations and time period—the rest of your story will reflect our modern world. On the other hand, any form of fantasy, science fiction, or even historical fiction will require a significant amount of worldbuilding. Not only will you need to explain the culture and settings of these worlds, but you'll also want to cover what kinds of technology and languages are present, what your fictional society thinks in terms of religion and social norms, et cetera.

At the end of the day, you may or may not cover every item on this list. Again, different stories will focus on different types of worldbuilding, so just record the elements that are most relevant to your novel. We'll be returning to these in a few days.

The Goals of Day Two

With a substantial portion of your reverse outline complete, we're officially done with Day Two. However, there's one more thing you might have come across while completing today's goals—the realization that the story you wrote isn't the story you set out to write.

This is a difficult reality that a lot of writers face when they begin the editing process, and it often manifests as a strange mix of frustration and confusion. You're hopefully proud of your first draft, at least on some level—I mean, you wrote a novel, and that's a big deal! Still, you may also feel like the story you ended up writing doesn't fully reflect the story you created in your head. Your settings and descriptions might not feel up to par, or your characters may fail to capture the complexity and depth you originally imagined.

To a large extent, this is the result of a gap between your skills and your imagination, and it's a common problem for all kinds of artists—our minds are almost always a few steps ahead of what our hands can create. Even if we can visualize what we want our story to become, we then have to translate that perfect vision into imperfect words. At the end of the day, this is a big part of what the editing process is all about —getting your novel closer in line with the story you see in your head. Still, no novel is perfect, no matter how much you edit or rewrite it.

To some extent, we have to accept that there will always be a gap between the story we have and the story we want, especially this early in the editing process. Your novel should get much closer to your vision as we move further into this challenge, but there will always be some level of disconnect. The best thing you can do at this stage is to accept that those flaws exist, allowing you to think clearly about the story you have—even as you work to turn it into the story you want.

Tomorrow we'll hone in on your individual scenes, but for now, here are the goals you've completed for Day Two:

1. Organize your novel's structure using the six core plot points of the Three Act Structure.
2. Summarize the events of each act in your story in one or two paragraphs.
3. Create in-depth character sheets for your core cast, paying special attention to those with character arcs.
4. List the rules of your story's world, along with any other important worldbuilding notes.

On to Day Three!

DAY THREE: HUNTING FOR HOTSPOTS

I f you've read many novels in your life, then you're bound to have encountered at least one whose story was frustratingly disconnected. Nothing about the novel seemed to mean anything, and few—if any—events genuinely impacted the adventure as a whole. Worst of all, because of these flaws I imagine you quickly lost interest in what was happening and, without a compelling reason to keep reading, you probably set that book down for good.

Unfortunately, most of us can think of more than just one novel that suffers from this problem. All too often authors become so entrenched in their own stories that, while *they* can see how it's all supposed to connect, they forget to make sure their *readers* can too. Which raises a question…

If they can't see the problems in their stories, how can you?

Well, for starters, this isn't some kind of mysterious curse we're forced to cross our fingers over and hope will pass us by. In reality, this lack of interconnectedness is just the sign of a poorly paced novel—and it's entirely curable!

While pacing impacts your story in a variety of ways, one of its primary roles is determining how engaging your novel is both moment-to-moment and overall. This means pacing is critically important to the success of your novel, and we'll be talking about it a lot over the next few days.

Today, however, our main focus will be twofold—what does your novel's pacing look like, and how can it be improved? We'll learn some fun editing techniques along the way, so pull out your highlighters and open up your reverse outline. We'll start with the basics.

The Basics of Scene Structure

Yesterday we made a lot of progress on your reverse outline, but there's still one important thing missing—your scene timeline.

If you're unfamiliar with what this means, a scene timeline is essentially a short breakdown of every scene in your novel, giving you a way to quickly see your story at a glance. This is a vital tool when it comes to analyzing your pacing, because it lets you see how your plot, character arcs, and story come together as a whole—a key component of good pacing.

Of course, as was the case yesterday, if you're following along from *The Ten Day Outline* you should already have most of this scene timeline complete. Still, don't gloss over this chapter right away. There will be a few extra things you'll want to add to your existing scene timeline, so skip to the next subsection and continue from there.

For those of you who don't have a preexisting scene timeline —or are unfamiliar with what scenes even are—let's start off with a quick explanation.

At their core, scenes are the building blocks of your novel, acting as the individual units your story is built from. Scenes are actually miniature stories themselves, and they follow a lot of the same principles of story structure that your larger novel does. However, unlike your novel, scenes follow a slightly abbreviated structure. This structure is comprised of six basic parts:

- **Goal:** Your characters are pursuing a goal.
- **Challenge:** They face various conflicts while trying to reach that goal.
- **Outcome:** There's an outcome, either positive or negative.
- **Reaction:** Your characters react to that outcome.
- **Reflection:** They consider their options going forward.
- **Decision (New Goal):** They make a decision, forming a new goal and beginning the cycle again.

These six parts are further divided into two distinct phases: Action and Reaction. The Action phase comes first, and is what you might normally think of as a scene. This phase contains the Goal, Challenges, and Outcome, and follows your characters as they pursue a goal, struggle against their enemies, make friends, and get themselves into trouble—essentially, the action of the scene. By the end of this phase, they'll have either achieved their goal, achieved it with unintended consequences, or failed to achieve it at all.

From there, the scene moves into the Reaction phase, consisting of Reaction, Reflection, and Decision. This phase is all about your characters reacting to the events they've just faced and making plans for what comes next, and the goal they develop in this Reaction phase will become the goal they pursue in the following scene. Perhaps what's most interesting about this second phase is that it can also vary wildly in length—some Reaction phases are only a sentence or two, while others contain entire monologues. Still, regardless of length the Reaction phase should always serve the same purpose—giving your characters a chance to reflect on what has happened, learn from it or fail to learn from it, and decide on their next goal.

When combined effectively, this basic scene structure creates a natural ebb and flow between your scenes. More importantly, it ensures all your scenes have some kind of connective tissue binding them together—every scene begins with the goal created in the previous scene for this reason.

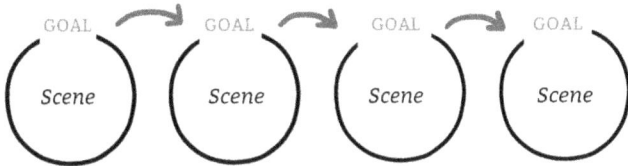

To see this scene structure at work, let's look at the opening scene of one of our example movies, *Princess Mononoke*:

- **Goal:** A creature is approaching Ashitaka's village, and it's his job to monitor it.
- **Challenges:** As the creature comes into view he realizes it's a demon. If he touches it he'll become cursed, which becomes a problem when it attacks him and his village.
- **Outcome:** Ashitaka jumps in front of the demon to protect three girls from his village. He's able to kill the creature, but it curses him in the process.

- **Reaction:** Ashitaka is in tremendous pain. He and others from his village struggle to heal the wound in whatever way they can.
- **Reflection:** As it lays dying, the demon warns the villagers and Ashitaka that they will suffer thanks to his hatred and grief. Ashitaka is afraid, and will need the support of his community to figure out his next steps.
- **Decision:** Ashitaka will consult with the elders of his village to see if there is any way to undo the curse.

If you're familiar with this movie, then you'll know that the Reaction phase of this scene is fairly short, less than a fourth of the scene in total. However, it sets up everything that comes next—as you would expect, Ashitaka begins the next scene by consulting with the leaders of his village, who send him away to break the curse and begin his journey.

It's this scene structure that will form the foundation of your novel's pacing, ensuring you not only have plenty of time to flesh out your plot, but to nurture your characters' inner journeys as well.

While this might sound overwhelming at first—especially if this is your first foray into scene structure—don't worry. For now, all you need to do is determine where the scenes in your own novel begin and end. We'll get into refining and polishing those scenes later on.

Building a Scene Timeline

With the basics of scene structure out of the way, we can move on to building your scene timeline. This should be a fairly straightforward process, but it will require you to flip through your manuscript a lot, so start by pulling that out.

Then, open to a blank page in your reverse outline and copy down the template below, leaving a blank line at the top:

- Goal:
- Challenges:
- Outcome:
- Reaction:
- Reflection:
- Decision:

This will be the foundation of your scene timeline, so you'll want to start by skimming through your story and picking out the individual scenes that make up your novel. As you go, mark where they begin and end in your manuscript and write them down in your timeline. Whenever you find a scene that contains one of the plot points we covered yesterday, make a note beside that scene's entry as well.

From there, write a short phrase that summarizes that scene in the blank space you left above each template. Then write that short phrase at the start of the scene in your manuscript itself. This will act as a title for that scene, making it easy to reference when you begin your rewrites later on. Personally, I even like to draw lines between where scenes begin and end so they stand out, but you can simply write each scene's name in the margins if you prefer.

If you ever find yourself struggling to figure out where your scenes begin and end, try focusing on your characters' goals. When they begin pursuing a new goal, that's likely the start of a new scene, and this can help you identify scenes much more quickly.

Keep going through this process until you have all of your scenes titled and marked in your manuscript. Then, return to the beginning of your novel and begin filling out the template you copied down earlier. Fill out that scene's Goal, Challenges, Outcome, Reaction, Reflection, and Decision, flipping back to the definitions we covered earlier as much as you need. If you simply can't figure out how a specific scene fits within this template, or if a scene is outright missing a piece of this structure, don't worry about it for now—just fill out whatever you can for each scene.

Alongside this template, there are two other things you'll want to include in your scene timeline, and this is where things will begin to differ from the timeline you may have created in *The Ten Day Outline*. For starters, transfer any scene-specific notes you took during your first reading to your timeline, organizing them beneath the appropriate scenes. Then, mark any scenes you feel need some work—for instance, ones with missing sections in your template—to return to later. Both of these things will come up tomorrow when you develop your game plan for rewriting your novel, and having them clearly organized by scene will make that process much, *much* easier.

Of course, throughout all of this I strongly encourage you to use shorthand. It's already quite a tedious process to flip through your manuscript over and over, and writing long paragraphs for each scene will only make the process take longer. Keep things short and sweet and instead focus on capturing the core events of each scene in your timeline.

Additionally, for those of you who are building off your preexisting timeline from *The Ten Day Outline*, don't skip these steps. Mark any problematic scene in your manuscript and check to see if the scenes you wrote still match the scenes you outlined in your original timeline. While everything may be the same, it's still well worth your time to double check now, so you don't run into any surprises later.

Finally, once you've finished outlining each scene in your novel, sit back and relax.

This is definitely a long process, but you'll soon see just how much time—and stress—it'll save you in the long run. Once your hand has had a rest and you're ready to continue, we can begin mapping these scenes and exploring how your novel's pacing comes together.

Mapping Your Story

With your scene timeline complete, it's time to get into the real fun of today's goals—story mapping.

Earlier in the chapter, I talked about how many authors fail to see the problems with their novel's pacing, even when those same problems are painfully clear to their readers. This is just one more way authors struggle to be objective about their own stories. They know how everything is *supposed* to connect, but this makes it hard to recognize when those connections aren't actually happening in the story itself—which is where story mapping comes in.

At its core, story mapping is a fairly simple process designed to help you understand your story's pacing in a more visual way. Basically, you'll be scanning through your scene timeline and marking each individual scene based on where it falls along three spectrums, with the end result being a color-coded map of your story's pacing. By the time you're done creating this map, your scene timeline should be sporting a rainbow of colors, which is perhaps the best part!

In total, we'll be mapping three different categories: Pacing, Conflict, and Character.

Pacing is pretty self-explanatory, and is all about analyzing the overall pace of your story—is it leaning more towards action, or reaction?

Conflict and Character are where things get a bit more complex. Specifically, Conflict is about identifying where the biggest developments of your plot occur, and Character is about finding the major moments of growth within your characters' arcs. This part of your story map will let you track how your plot and characters are developing, with an eye towards finding one specific thing: hotspots.

Hotspots are points within your story where you see a sudden spike of activity, usually from a combination of both major plot and character developments. Ideally, hotspots should also align with your story's structure, appearing in clusters around major plot points like the First Plot Point or the Midpoint. This is because, at their core, your novel's plot and characters should be intimately connected. As your protagonist grows and changes along their journey, they should influence how your plot develops. Likewise, as your plot marches forward, it should challenge and shape your characters in new ways. This is how you know the most important elements of your story are interconnected, and how you can tell whether your plot and characters are working in harmony. Throw good overall pacing into the mix, with a satisfying balance of action and reflection-dominant scenes, and you'll have a story that delivers readers a compelling journey—one they'll struggle to put down.

So, to start mapping your own story, you'll first need a key. Look through your collection of pens and pencils and pick out different colors for these five things:

- Action-dominant scenes
- Reaction-dominant scenes
- Major developments in your core conflict
- Major developments in your subplots
- Major developments in a protagonist's character arc
- Major developments in your core characters' arcs

As you choose your colors, record them in your reverse outline so you know what each one means. Personally, I even go so far as to keep my colors for each category within a similar scheme, such as reds and pinks for conflict or light blues and greens for character arcs. However, feel free to use whatever combination of colors feels most intuitive to you— the goal is to create a key you can easily understand at a glance, regardless of what that might look like. The same goes for what writing utensils you use. Highlighters, colored pencils, or markers work great, as does the highlighting function of most modern word processors.

Once you've chosen your colors, you can begin mapping each of these categories onto your scene timeline. We'll start with Pacing first, since this should be the easiest to complete:

———

Pacing:

To map your story's pacing, go through your scene timeline and mark each scene as either action-dominant or reaction-dominant using the key you created. Of course, we literally just talked about how each scene you write should have both an Action and Reaction phase, so how does this work?

Well, though each scene in your story should contain a bit of both, the majority of your scenes will lean heavily in one direction or the other. If the bulk of the scene involves your characters facing off against major conflicts, then mark that scene as action-dominant. On the other hand, if the scene is more concerned with your characters' inner growth, their plans for the future, their thoughts on the past, or other emotional challenges, then it's a reaction-dominant scene.

———

As you go about mapping your scenes' pacing, you'll likely wonder what kind of balance your story should have between action and reaction-dominant scenes—and for the most part, this will depend on your novels genre.

For instance, adventures, westerns, and thrillers all tend to be action-dominant, simply because of their action-oriented nature. Action dominant-scenes have a faster, more energetic feel thanks to their greater focus on plot and conflict, while reaction-dominant scenes will feel slower and more introspective. Because of this, romances, literary novels, and speculative fiction tend to skew the other way, often being strongly reaction-dominant thanks to their greater focus on character development.

Of course, there will always be exceptions to these rules, and all stories—regardless of genre—should strive to strike a healthy balance in their pacing.

To understand what I mean, it can help to think of your novel's pacing as a funnel. The widest and slower-paced portions of your story will be at the top of the funnel, or the beginning of your novel, slowly narrowing and speeding up as you approach the end. This is because the beginning of your novel has more room for exploration of both your story's world and characters, while the very end of your novel should focus on driving the plot forward towards the Climax, rather than introducing new things.

Still, regardless of where you are in your novel, you want to strike a balance between both action-dominant and reaction-dominant scenes. A huge string of action-dominant scenes all back to back will feel rushed and exhausting for your reader, while nothing but reflection dominant scenes chapter after chapter can make your story drag. Both serve an important role in your novel, and you'll need a blend of both regardless of your genre. If you find that your story has a lot of sections with just one type of scene or the other, make a note of those in your scene timeline—we'll continue dealing with these pacing issues tomorrow.

From there, you can move on to mapping the Conflict and Character categories. This is where hotspots will really come into play, and you'll hopefully find that you're marking a lot of activity close together in your story. Of course, don't let that sway your decisions at this stage—make sure you're marking scenes that genuinely fulfill the requirements of each category:

———

Conflict:

To map your story's Conflict, start by scanning through your scene timeline and looking for any scenes that feature major developments or turning points in your core conflict. You'll hopefully find that most of these overlap with the plot points you identified earlier on, so those are a good place to begin your search.

When assessing whether or not a scene has a major impact on your core conflict, think back to your Dramatic Question from Day One. How does this scene affect that question and does it change what your reader believes the outcome might be? How does it impact the plot of your novel as a whole?

Of course, some scenes will feature setbacks for your protagonist, while others will see them succeeding. Both of these can impact your core conflict equally, so mark them the same way.

Alongside marking these scenes, you'll also want to mark scenes with major developments for your subplots or secondary conflicts as well—if you have any. These should follow the same principle as your core conflict, just focused on that particular subplot instead. If the scene drives that subplot forward, either in a positive or negative way, mark it in your timeline with the appropriate color from your key.

Once you're done mapping both your core conflict and your subplots, take a few notes about any problems or concerns you might have—such as not having enough scenes that impact your core conflict, or only having these scenes isolated to one part of your novel.

Character:

To begin mapping the Character category, start by focusing on your protagonist. Reference their character arc from your character sheet and scan through your scene timeline. Mark any major developments along their arc, or any moments when they undergo a lot of growth.

For instance, if we were mapping the scenes in Disney's *Mulan*, you'd mark the scene where Mulan steals her father's armor and sneaks away to join the Chinese army in his stead. This scene is a pivotal moment within her character arc, and features a major and difficult decision that starts her down the path she'll follow for the rest of the story. You might also mark the scene when her fellow soldiers discover she is a woman and abandon her in the mountains—this is the darkest moment along her arc and makes her deeply question if she did the right thing.

Now, go through your own scene timeline and look for similar scenes for your protagonist. Just like when mapping your Conflict, you'll likely find that these major character moments overlap with your story's plot points in some way. These are a good place to look if you're having trouble nailing down what scenes carry the most impact within your protagonist's character arc.

Once you've finished marking the major character moments for your protagonist, pick one or two other core characters from your story and do the same for them. Look for scenes that deeply impact their character arcs, remembering to mark them with the appropriate color. When you're done with both, take a few notes about what you've found and how you feel about the results.

———

By the time you've finished marking your scenes based on these two categories, your scene timeline should have a decent rainbow of colors spread across it.

Ideally, you'll find that most of these colors are clustered around the plot points you identified yesterday. That means these plot points are acting as hotspots within your story, which is exactly what you want—these plot points should feature the biggest turning points of your novel, combining major developments within both your core conflict and your protagonist's arc. If these scenes are also influencing your secondary plots and characters, all the better!

The end result of these hotspots will be scenes that feel deeply meaningful within your story as a whole, tying together the many threads that make up your novel.

Of course, these hotspots may be spread across multiple scenes. For instance, it's not uncommon for major moments in your conflict to happen during action-dominant scenes, with the following reaction-dominant scene focusing on major character developments—somewhat like a duet. Either way, this will still have the same effect.

Ultimately, creating hotspots that connect your story's structure, conflict, and characters is one of the surest ways to keep your readers engaged and satisfied with your story. However, you may find that there aren't many hotspots in your story quite yet—in which case, don't panic. As with so much of the work we've done these last few days, we're still in the analysis phase. The rewrite phase will be coming very soon, and that's when you'll get to iron out any of the problems you've discovered over the last few days, regardless of what they may be.

The Goals of Day Three

With your scene timeline complete and your story mapped, you've finished the bulk of your reverse outline. You've also probably developed a pretty large collection of notes to sift through—this is completely normal, and dealing with these problems will be the entire focus of tomorrow's goals.

For now, I hope today has helped you see your story's pacing more clearly. As we talked about at the start of today's chapter, pacing is one of those things that's easy to lose sight of within your own novel. After spending so much time immersed in your story, it becomes harder and harder to see how your scenes actually connect on the page—everything makes sense in your head, even if it doesn't for your readers.

Fortunately, by the end of today you should have a much clearer picture of how your novel works, meaning you're that much closer to fixing those problems come tomorrow!

Tomorrow you'll develop your editing game plan, but for now, here are the goals you've completed for Day Three:

1. Create a scene timeline for your story, marking each scene in your manuscript as you go.
2. Add any notes you took during your first reading to your scene timeline.
3. Map your story's pacing by marking scenes as either action-dominant or reflection-dominant.
4. Finish your story map by labeling your scenes based on how they affect your novel's conflict and characters.

On to Day Four!

5

DAY FOUR: YOUR PLAN OF ATTACK

There's a saying in the programming world that, "the sooner you start coding, the longer it will take." Basically, without a plan to guide you you'll end up working yourself into a corner, spending far more time on the project than if you had gone in with a clear idea from the start.

While at first glance this may seem unrelated to the topic of this book—after all, we aren't building web applications here —this basic principle actually applies to a whole variety of disciplines, including writing. There's a reason I've talked about the importance of building a robust outline so often throughout this series. Having a plan simply makes life easier, allowing you to stay oriented towards your goals even when things get difficult.

Still, planning and organization don't always *feel* like progress, no matter how vital they are. Believe it or not, you're approaching the halfway point of this challenge, yet I imagine you don't feel like you've gotten much done—yes, you've created a reverse outline, but you've yet to actually change anything in your story itself.

All of that changes after today.

While everything up to this point has served to help you better understand your story, today is when you'll finally decide how to actually fix that story's flaws and bolster its strengths. Though I know you're itching to start revising your draft and polishing your novel, bear with me for one more day—by the end of today, you'll have a solid plan to guide you going forward, meaning you won't waste any time as you finally put all your hard work into action.

Understanding Your Plot

We've covered a ton of topics over the last few days, including everything from story structure, to character development and scene structure. That's a lot to process in such a short time, and I imagine it was hard to see how all of those different elements of storytelling actually affected your own novel.

What do you need to do to improve *your* story?

That'll be our primary focus for today. Throughout the rest of this chapter, I'll be walking you through a little over forty questions split among five categories designed to help you tackle each and every piece of your first draft. These will help you understand how to apply everything you've learned about your story thus far, and your answers will be used to craft a game plan covering what needs to be changed, where, and when—basically, a to-do list for revising your draft!

The first of these five categories will be your plot.

What I'll do is ask you two to five questions at a time and then explain the thought behind them to guide you as you answer each one. As we go, make sure to take plenty of notes about your thought process and record your answers in your reverse outline. We'll be revisiting these answers at the end of the chapter.

- Does your story start at the right time?
- Does it end at the right time?
- Does the beginning of the story set up the ending?
- Does the beginning of your story set the right expectations for your reader?

First up, let's deal with the skeleton of your story.

The beginning of your novel sets the stage for everything that's to come, so getting it right is vital to the health of your story. The biggest problem most writers make here is starting their story at the wrong time—either they start too close to the First Plot Point, not giving themselves enough time to introduce their story's world, or they start too far away, causing Act 1 to drag and lose the reader's interest.

This is a delicate balance to strike, but a good way to identify the right time for your story to start is by asking whether or not the beginning of your novel sets up the ending.

Does it set the right expectations for your reader?

The very first scene your readers experience should hint at the conflict to come, setting the tone for the rest of the adventure they're about to go on. This is a promise you're making, telling your readers what kind of story they're about to experience, and you want to make sure you're making a promise you can keep. In a similar vein, you also want the opening scene of your novel to relate to the ending—what is the Climax of your story, and how does your opening scene put your characters on a path towards that Climax?

While it's always important to introduce your characters and their ordinary world throughout Act 1, by laying the groundwork of your novel's conflict in the very first scene you make it that much more compelling for your reader to keep reading. And, of course, you definitely don't want to start your novel by introducing a problem you won't actually resolve by the end—this not only betrays that promise you made to your readers, but it's also just bad writing.

From there, once you've decided when your story will start, you also need to make sure it ends in the right place too.

Endings can suffer from many of the same problems as beginnings—too short and they feel rushed, too long and they become dull and boring. As a general rule, once your Climax reaches its end you should move quickly through the Resolution before wrapping up your novel. Hit the high notes and show how this wild adventure has affected your story's world and characters, hinting at what comes next in their lives before moving on. The worst thing a Resolution can do is drag on too long, sucking the emotional energy out of the finale of the story—just look at the four separate endings in the final *Lord of the Rings* movie and you'll see what I mean.

While you want to give your reader time to appreciate everything they've gone through with your cast, your story should always end when their emotions are still high after the intensity of the Climax.

- Is the core conflict of your story clearly identified?
- Does this conflict matter to your story's world?
- Does each section of your story affect this conflict?
- Are you exploring this conflict in enough depth?
- Does this conflict escalate as the story progresses?

As I'm sure you can tell based on the questions above, your novel's conflict is *important*.

Not only will it shape every aspect of your plot, but it will also be what drives your reader to keep reading and your characters to keep moving forward. A story without conflict isn't a story at all—this is why making sure your novel's conflict is as strong as possible should be at the very top of your to-do list.

Like I mentioned previously, readers should have at least some idea of what core conflict will drive your story by the end of your very first scene, even if this is only a vague idea at first. For instance, *Mulan* opens with the start of the Hun invasion, just like *Star Wars: A New Hope* opens with an attack on Princess Leia's ship and *How to Train Your Dragon* opens with dragons raiding Berk. Each of these opening scenes immediately establish that there are problems afoot, giving the rest of the story room to build on that conflict until it reaches its peak.

Of course, this conflict won't be very compelling if it doesn't truly matter within the context of your story. Small-scale conflicts aren't a bad thing, but your story's conflict should still have a genuine effect on your protagonist, regardless of its size—if it can affect their community and the world around them as well, all the better.

This also means that every, and I mean *every*, part of your novel should tie back into this core conflict in some way. While there's nothing wrong with exploring subplots, there should always be the simmering undercurrent of your core conflict present. If that conflict isn't playing a role in every scene of your novel, even if it's just a small one, then that conflict either isn't strong enough to support your whole story or that scene is extraneous to the story you're telling.

Finally, ask yourself—how well do you expand on your core conflict? Do you go beyond the surface level and show how it truly impacts your cast and their world? Likewise, how does your novel's conflict grow more intense and impactful as your story develops?

You should always be driving your characters towards the Climax of your novel, and to do that your core conflict needs to steadily increase in both urgency and tension—to up the ante, so to speak. The noose has to tighten around your characters' necks to push them into action *and* to keep your readers invested in what's happening on the page.

- Does your story's plot feature turning points in the right places?
- How strong is your Hook, First Plot Point, Midpoint, Third Plot Point, Climax, and Resolution?

These next two questions are all about your story's structure —how well is your novel structured, and how can it be improved?

For starters, you'll want to look at where each of your plot points fall within your story. When you do, you may find a variety of things. Perhaps Act 1 is too long, or Act 3 is way too short. Maybe your plot points are in all the wrong places. While your Midpoint doesn't need to fall exactly halfway through your novel, you do want it to occur roughly in the middle. Likewise, your First Plot Point should happen around a quarter of the way through your story, your Third Plot Point around three quarters, and your Climax and Resolution at the very end.

Though it might seem restrictive, these turning points aren't placed arbitrarily. Not only do they ensure you have enough time to fully explore your plot and characters, but they keep your story moving forward at a consistent pace. While your story doesn't have to match these timings exactly, you want it to get close.

From there, you can start considering how strong these plot points are to begin with. Is your Hook a bit lacking, or maybe your Resolution? Worse yet, do you not have a Hook at all? You want all six of these plot points to be represented within your novel, so if you're missing any, tweaking scenes or adding news ones should be your first order of business. Then, revisit the requirements for each plot point from Day Two and ask yourself if the scenes you've chosen fulfill them to the fullest. Remember that your protagonist should be the primary driver of change during these turning points as well, and should be genuinely affected by whatever happens.

As frustrating as it may be to realize your first draft is lacking in terms of story structure, and as tempting as it may be to skip these two questions, I don't include them just for fun. Again, these plot points aren't arbitrary—each one serves a very distinct role within your novel, and without all six your whole story becomes fragile. While you don't need to uproot your vision for your story by any means, taking the time to consider each of these structural elements and how you can incorporate them will only strengthen your novel as a whole.

- How does your plot tie into your theme?
- Have you taken care of any necessary foreshadowing in earlier scenes?

Finally, these last two questions are more open-ended. How you handle your story's theme and foreshadowing will really depend on the novel you're writing, meaning there's not as much specific guidance for me to share. Still, let's take a moment to consider them before moving on.

Do you have a theme in mind for your novel, and how does your plot play into that theme? Ideally, your theme should be something you can easily boil down into just a few words. For example, *Mulan's* theme is self worth, while *Princess Mononoke* focuses on themes of natural harmony. Whatever your theme is, take a moment to ponder it and see if your story really speaks to that theme—if not, you'll either want to change the theme you're thinking of, or tweak your story.

Last but not least, foreshadowing.

This can be a pain to deal with simply because of how challenging it is to pull off, but that doesn't mean it isn't worth paying attention to. Much like the opening scene of your novel makes a promise to your reader about the kind of story they're about to experience, your foreshadowing makes a promise that something is brewing within your conflict. Consider the major plot developments within your novel— do you hint at them early on, or at least set the stage for them before they happen?

After all, you want your reader to say, "Wow, I didn't see that coming," rather than, "Where did that come from?"

Studying Your Characters

With plot out of the way, let's move on to your characters.

These two categories are fairly interconnected, so you'll likely find some overlap between these next questions and the ones we just covered. Still, take notes on any thoughts you have or problems you find so we can add them to your to-do list in just a bit.

- Does your protagonist change by the end of your story, or affect a significant change in others?
- What is your protagonist's deepest flaw, and how does your story force them to grow past that flaw?
- Does your protagonist have a personal goal driving them forward?
- How does your protagonist shape the direction of your plot?

In terms of your cast, your protagonist will have by far the biggest role to play throughout your novel. Not only should they be the primary driver of change within your plot, but your readers will be invested in their growth and happiness. As an author, you want to deliver on that growth, so ensuring your protagonist has a strong character arc is vital. Of course, to have a character arc your protagonist will need to experience at least some level of change between the beginning and the end of your novel—the only exception to this rule is with flat arc characters.

To understand how your protagonist changes throughout their arc, you'll first want to figure out where they start. What is their deepest flaw, and how does your story challenge them to grow beyond that flaw? By the end, your protagonist should be in a different place both emotionally and mentally compared to where they began, and your plot should have played an active role in bringing about that change—though this change could be either positive or negative, depending on their character arc. If you're still unsure what arc your protagonist follows, go back and reference our explanation of character arcs from Day Two.

Once you know how your protagonist will change from the beginning of their adventure to the end, you can shift focus to their goal. Every character in your novel needs a goal to shape their actions and behavior, and your protagonist is no exception. In fact, their goal will carry even more weight because of their central role in your novel.

Unfortunately, this is where many writers get tripped up. You see, your protagonist's goal needs to be personal, not simply to solve the core conflict of your plot. Let's look at our four example movies to see this in action:

- *Mulan:* Mulan's goal is to make her family proud.
- *How to Train Your Dragon:* Hiccup's goal is to earn his father's respect.
- *A New Hope:* Luke's goal is to go on an adventure.
- *Princess Mononoke:* Ashitaka's goal is to lift his curse.

Each of these personal goals exist outside the core conflict of their respective stories and, more importantly, they shape how these protagonists respond to that conflict. While handling the core conflict is important to these characters, it is *not* the only goal that drives them forward—instead, their involvement in these core conflicts is largely the result of them pursuing their personal goals.

- *Mulan:* Mulan joins the army to protect her father and prove she can be useful to her family.
- *How to Train Your Dragon:* Hiccup shoots down and ultimately befriends a dragon after trying to kill it to earn his father's approval.
- *A New Hope:* Luke gets involved in the rebel cause after setting out on his adventure with Obi-Wan.
- *Princess Mononoke:* Ashitaka ends up stuck in the middle of a war between nature and humans while trying to find a cure for his curse.

Your protagonist should have a similarly powerful personal goal pushing them forward outside the strict confines of your novel's conflict.

While solving your core conflict will eventually become one of their goals, they still need something personal to shape their actions and to provide an extra layer of depth to their character. Of course, that means this personal goal should stick with them throughout your novel, only reaching its conclusion at the end—otherwise, you aren't using it to its fullest potential.

Finally, your protagonist needs to shape the direction of your novel's plot. Their actions should determine how your core conflict develops, and other characters should have to react to their choices. This is especially true after the Midpoint, when they'll take a more active role in pursuing your story's conflict and antagonist.

Basically, if your protagonist is just tagging along for the ride, never stepping up to shape their own story, then they probably shouldn't be your protagonist to begin with.

- Are there any characters that serve the same purpose, or no purpose at all?
- Do all of your core characters play a role at multiple points throughout your story?
- Do all of your core characters have a goal to pursue and does this goal influence their actions?
- Does your antagonist have their own goals and motivations beyond your protagonist?

Shifting our focus to the rest of your cast, one of the next things you'll need to consider is whether or not you have any characters that are extraneous.

While you don't need to be too vicious about cutting excess characters, you still want all of your named characters to serve some kind of purpose within your story. Maybe they're a mentor figure, or perhaps they help your antagonist gain the upper hand before the Third Plot Point. Perhaps they're pivotal to expanding on your worldbuilding, or maybe they lend a sympathetic ear to your protagonist in a time of need. Whatever their role is, each character in your story needs at least one—and this is even more true for your core cast.

Finally, all of your characters—just like your protagonist— need a goal to pursue. Again, this is especially true for your core cast, since they'll be a more consistent presence within your story and will need stronger motivations as a result.

In particular, this is extra important for your antagonist. Just like your protagonist's personal goal shouldn't only be to solve the core conflict, your antagonist needs a goal beyond just foiling the protagonist. If your protagonist never existed, what would your antagonist's goal be? While they'll certainly butt heads with your protagonist before the story ends, they need their own desires and motivations for your protagonist to stand in the way of, rather than their sole purpose being to thwart your protagonist's happiness.

- Are your characters' actions consistent with who they are as people?
- Do your characters move and change outside the immediate scope of your story?

As you got further into writing your first draft, your own voice may have started to overwhelm otherwise strong characters. This is easy to do, and to a large extent comes down to writing fatigue. While you may have been very aware of your character's individual personalities at the start of your draft, once you're tens of thousands of words in that extra bit of brain power is simply needed elsewhere.

Because of this, it's wise to take a moment to review how you've written your characters, especially towards the end of your draft. Are they still consistent with their own unique personalities, and do they have their own voice?

Likewise, remember that your novel is only a single slice of what's happening within your story's world. While you're off following your protagonist's adventures in one corner of your story, other characters should still be living their lives and making plans elsewhere. Time doesn't stop as soon as the camera pans away, so make sure the rest of your cast is still active when your protagonist is doing other things—even if this never shows up in your story itself, it's a good mental exercise at the very least!

- How do your characters tie into your theme?
- What is the emotional arc of your story?

Finally, we're going to be wrapping up this category with two, more difficult questions.

Just like your plot should tie into the theme of your novel, your characters should as well—especially your protagonist. Consider their character arcs and the lessons they learn throughout your story, and how those might relate back to the theme of your novel. While your whole cast doesn't need to learn the same lesson, by having multiple characters learn lessons that build off a single theme, your whole story will feel more thematically consistent and powerful.

For example, Hiccup from *How to Train Your Dragon* learns to value his unique skills and perspectives, while his father learns to respect that not everyone has to think like he does.

Both of these lessons tie into the plot of the movie which sees Hiccup struggling to convince the Vikings to accept a new way of life, likewise tying into the story's theme of acceptance. Because these elements are linked, the story becomes a single cohesive experience, carrying far more emotional impact than it would have otherwise.

Of course, this all ties into one final element—the emotional arc of your story.

This is much like your protagonist's arc, but for your story as a whole—where does your story begin emotionally, and where does it end? For instance, Mulan's story begins on a note of isolation and sadness. She's struggling to live up to her society's expectations, and views herself as a failure just for being herself. However, by the end of the movie we see the Emperor of China bow to her in respect, drawing a sharp parallel between where she started and where she ends. *Mulan* ends in a truly different place than it begins, with its protagonist returning home proud, strong, and finally realizing that her family loved her all along.

This is a powerful emotional arc that carries the movie as a whole, and it's worth thinking about how you could strike a similar contrast in your own novel. At the end of the day, what it all comes down to is where the emotions of your story begin, and where they end.

Fleshing Out Your World

Your plot and characters are by far the biggest categories you'll consider today, but that doesn't mean there aren't a few other elements of your draft to take care of.

First up, your worldbuilding.

- Does your story consistently follow its own rules?
- Do those rules feel believable in this world?

These two questions both focus on one simple problem— many stories aren't consistent with their worldbuilding, and readers can't suspend their disbelief as a result. Fortunately, this comes with an equally simple fix, and it's why we took the time to create your story's rulebook back on Day Two.

All you need to do is review that rulebook and make sure your story sticks to the rules you've set. If it deviates at any point, you either need to change that scene, change the rule, or have a *very* good explanation for why the rules of your story's world have suddenly shifted. Of course, consider how strong the logic of these rules are as well. This will naturally be harder the more you deviate from reality, but there are still plenty of science fiction and fantasy novels with deeply believable fictional worlds. The key is making sure your worldbuilding feels consistent, while also thinking through the majority of your readers' questions.

- Do you help your readers suspend their disbelief?
- Do you take enough time to introduce your reader to your story's world?

Similarly, all of your excellent worldbuilding will be wasted if you don't do enough to share it with your reader.

To a large extent, this just comes down to how you introduce your story's world, and this is where Act 1 and Act 2 really get their time to shine. Both give you space to explore your story's worldbuilding, while expanding on your characters and their goals at the same time. Of course, even when you're elaborating on your worldbuilding, make sure there's always some kind of conflict driving the scene forward—a scene that does nothing but explain facts about your story's world isn't really a scene, after all.

- Are there any elements of your worldbuilding that are worth elaborating on?
- Are you reusing the same handful of locations over and over, or are you exploring a variety of locations?

Continuing with this category's theme, these questions are all about making sure your worldbuilding has enough depth to support your story.

As with all forms of worldbuilding, this will be easier for stories grounded in the modern world, but that doesn't mean it isn't important even if you're writing in a less fantastical genre. You should always take a moment to review your story's rulebook and ensure your worldbuilding goes beyond surface level. Ask yourself—could you expand on this world by exploring things like its history, cultures, religions, foods, traditions, technologies, languages, et cetera?

This goes for settings, too. If your entire story takes place in the same handful of locations, it could be well worth your time to think of ways to introduce new sights and sounds to your story. It isn't necessarily bad to reuse locations, so long as you're adding new elements and details whenever you revisit them.

- Are you relying on cliches or stereotypes in your worldbuilding?
- Have you done your homework to ensure you truly understand the locations and people you're writing about?

Finally, before you wrap up your worldbuilding, you want to consider whether or not you're relying on cliches to tell your story. Worse yet, are you using stereotypes to describe people or places, ignoring what makes those groups unique? A big part of avoiding this is making sure you're introducing something interesting and novel to your worldbuilding, rather than leaning on the tropes we've all seen before.

Yet, there's another layer to this issue that comes down to honesty and sensitivity—stereotypes paint groups of people as "others," nothing more than flat caricatures that don't come close to capturing the real uniqueness we all represent. If you're writing about real locations or people, make sure you've done everything you can to understand that groups' culture and traditions from *their perspective,* instead of only leaning on stereotypes.

This goes for fictional worlds too!

Think about what cultural signals your fictional races or civilizations are sending—you may be surprised to find that you're drawing heavily from modern stereotypes, perhaps without even realizing it. While this isn't necessarily a bad thing, always do it with care and empathy, and consider adding a few of your own unique elements to take the place of these tropes.

Refining Your Story's Pace

We talked a lot about pacing yesterday, so you'll hopefully be able to answer these questions pretty quickly. Still, there may be a few that stump you, so let's go through them together.

- Do your major moments of conflict and character development overlap?

- Does your story have hotspots around your First Plot Point, Midpoint, Third Plot Point, and Climax?
- Do you have large chunks of action-dominant or reflection-dominant scenes?
- Do you narrow your protagonist's options throughout your story until they're on a crash course for the Climax?

These first few questions are all about analyzing the hotspots you found on Day Three, so take a moment to pull out your story map.

Ideally, you should find the bulk of your hotspots clustered around your First Plot Point, Midpoint, Third Plot Point, and Climax, though these will likely range in intensity. If any of these plot points are missing major moments of conflict or character development, that's something you'll definitely want to address in your game plan.

Usually, conflict isn't the problem here, since these turning points will naturally involve some level of conflict thanks to your plot—instead, it's getting major moments of character development to align at these plot points that can prove more difficult.

Fortunately, character arcs and story structure actually have a lot of overlap!

You see, your First Plot Point should be the moment your protagonist's arc really starts moving, while the Midpoint will see them make major progress in their growth. Similarly, the Third Plot Point will be a moment of darkness and struggle, while the Climax will either have them overcome their flaws and complete their arc, or end as a negative arc character. Either way, all of these plot points have a corresponding influence on your protagonist's arc.

You can see this at work in the graph below, which is a combination of the character arc and story structure charts we looked at back on Day Two:

CHARACTER ARCS AND THE THREE ACT STRUCTURE

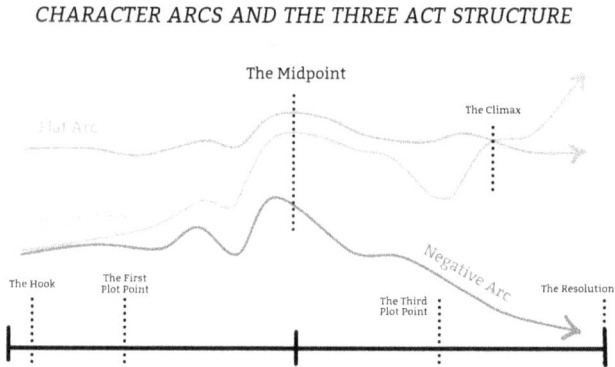

While these major moments of conflict and character development don't need to overlap perfectly within the same scene, try to have them form hotspots within consecutive scenes whenever possible.

From there, check to make sure you don't have any long stretches of scenes that are either all action-dominant or all reaction-dominant. Though there's nothing wrong with focusing on one or the other, you want to strike a balance by including the occasional outlier, preventing your scenes from feeling monotonous.

Finally, make sure your protagonist's options are narrowing more and more as you approach the Climax. Remember, your pacing should form the shape of a funnel, pushing your protagonist forward and increasing the tension as you march towards your finale.

- Is your story complete, or are there areas you still need to expand on?
- Are there any unnecessary or extraneous sections of your story?

We've covered the biggest issues in terms of your novel's pacing, but there are still a few smaller things to consider—specifically, whether or not your story feels complete, and whether there are any scenes that you should cut completely.

Your answers to both of these questions will largely depend on your novel and the scope of its conflict. However, a good way to test this is by asking yourself whether you've explored the full potential of your story. Do you resolve the problems you introduce in the beginning and does it feel like your story has meaningfully changed by the end?

A series will of course follow one conflict that ties multiple books together, but that doesn't mean meaningful progress shouldn't be made in each individual story. For standalone novels, this is even easier.

Likewise, all the scenes in your novel should serve a purpose related to this core conflict. If not, ask yourself what the point of that scene is, and consider either rewriting it to strengthen that conflict or removing it entirely.

- Is your story the right length?

Finally, the question of length.

This is a difficult question to answer because, again, a lot will depend on your unique story. What genre is it in, what subject matter does it tackle, how complex is your plot, and what kind of experience do you want to create?

At the end of the day, I strongly believe your novel's length should be more about telling a cohesive story without a lot of excess, rather than sticking to genre conventions or outside expectations. If your story is complete, then the length of your novel is probably right where it should be. The only good reason to change this is if you know there is a lot more ground to explore, or if you've wandered away from your core plot and need to trim the story back.

In the end, this is something you have to trust your gut on.

Choosing Your Point of View

Last but not least, you'll want to make sure the point of view you've of your novel suits the story you're trying to tell.

- Does your point of view serve your story's needs?
- Does your story's point of view suit your genre?
- How would changing your story's point of view affect how you tell your story and what information is available to the reader?
- Does your story's current point of view offer you enough flexibility to tell your story the way you want to?

Usually the point of view you wrote your first draft in will be just fine for your final novel—it's rare that I encourage writers to rewrite their entire draft, just to change their point of view. Still, it is possible that your story may be better served by a different point of view.

In case you've forgotten between discussing it now and back on Day One, there are four types of point of view commonly used in fiction:

- **First Person POV:** The entire story is told by your protagonist, using "I did/thought/felt/saw/etc…"
- **Peripheral First Person POV:** This is the same as First Person POV, except the narrator is not the protagonist.
- **Limited Third Person POV:** Here the narrator is not a character in the story at all, but an outside observer who follows the experiences of a single character. The story is told using "he/she/they."
- **Omniscient Third Person POV:** This POV uses "he/she/they" as well, but is not limited to any single character's experiences. This narrator can recount all of the events and experiences of every character in the story without limit.

Of course, the point of view you choose isn't just a stylistic choice—it'll affect how you tell your story as well.

For instance, First Person points of view are much more intimate, emotional, and personal, while Third Person points of view function more like a movie camera, lending the story a cinematic feel. Because of this, First Person is far more common in young adult fiction, romance novels, and other similar genres, while Third Person is often found in thrillers, fantasy, and science fiction.

Really, if you're unsure what point of view is best for your story, the easiest way to decide is by thinking of your reader. What type of experience do you want them to have—an intimate one, or a cinematic one? Likewise, what is your novel's greatest strength—your characters and their inner struggles, or your worldbuilding and plot? If it's the former of either of these, then First Person is probably your best choice. If it's the latter, consider Third Person.

Your Finished Game Plan

With all of those questions out of the way, we're almost done with today's goals. All that's left now is to condense your notes into an organized game plan that you can put into action as you revise your draft. To get started, flip to a blank page in your reverse outline and write down these four sections:

- Act 1
- Act 2
- Act 3
- All

Now, take a moment to review everything you wrote today, along with your reverse outline as a whole. This will give you one more chance to refamiliarize yourself with everything going on in your story, including any notes you took earlier on in the challenge. As you go, transfer these notes to one of the four sections you just created, depending on what part of your story they affect. Label them as either plot, character, worldbuilding, pacing, or point of view as well.

For example, if I noticed that my protagonist had no strong personal goal in Act 1, I would write that note beneath the Act 1 section and label it "characters." On the other hand, if I had made a note about point of view that affected the story as a whole, I would put it under All.

Once you've organized these notes beneath their appropriate sections, review what you've written—is there any overlap between the problems you identified today and the notes you took earlier on in the challenge? If not, are those earlier notes still problems you want to fix within your story? If they aren't, feel free to cross them out.

Finally, with all of your notes organized, you can turn them into a to-do list for tomorrow.

Start by going through each section of notes and consider how you can turn that flaw or problem into a specific change within your story. Some of these will be fairly easy, like starting your story in a later scene, while others will take more time and consideration. Don't panic if you're having trouble—you already know what needs to be fixed, meaning all you need to do now is take your time and brainstorm the best ways to apply that fix to your story.

Once you've gone through all of your notes and turned each one into an item on your to-do list, you're officially done with today's goals.

The Goals of Day Four

With Day Four behind us, I feel safe in saying that this is one of the most mentally demanding days of this challenge.

We've covered so much material, and a lot of it was pretty complex. Still, by the end of today you should have a clear idea of what comes next for your story, along with a plan for how you'll put your fixes into action. That's a good feeling, and it's always at this point in the challenge that I can finally start seeing my novels coming together.

Even though you haven't applied any of your fixes quite yet, you can rest easy knowing you have everything on hand for when you're ready to tackle your rewrites. We aren't done with this challenge for a while yet, but your story will only continue to improve from here.

I hope you're excited about what's to come!

Tomorrow you'll take your first break, but for now, here are the goals you've completed for Day Four:

1. Using your reverse outline, answer a set of questions to determine what revisions your story needs.
2. Organize those revisions into a game plan, separated by Act 1, Act 2, Act 3, and All.
3. Add any notes you've taken throughout the challenge beneath their appropriate section.
4. Review your proposed revisions and turn them into a list of to-dos.

On to the First Rest!

6

THE FIRST REST

B y now, it should be no secret that every novel is unique
—though we're all on the same path, the stories we're
creating are solely our own.

For the most part, that individual experience is a wonderful
thing, giving us the space to dream up amazing tales and
adventures no one else could! However, it also means
everyone's editing journey will be a bit different, and I won't
hide it—that fact was hard to account for when developing
this challenge. While outlining a novel and writing a first
draft are both fairly straightforward tasks, editing comes
with so many unknowable twists and turns unique to each
person. It was a long time before I figured out how to handle
that. Fortunately, the answer was hidden in plain sight all
along, and it comes in the form of the First Rest.

You see, the First Rest acts as a pause within this ten day
challenge, putting your normal goals on hold while you take
the time you need to put Day Four's game plan into action.
In fact, beyond working your way through your game plan

and taking a few notes as you go, there are no other goals for this chapter—which brings up an important question:

Why isn't this rest part of the normal ten day process?

Well, while it *is* possible you'll be able to finish all of your rewrites in a single day, it's also very possible you won't be. As I said, your story is unique, and that means the state of your first draft will be unique as well. You may be lucky, and your draft may only need a few minor tweaks before it's brought up to speed. However, it's just as likely that you have some major rewrites ahead of you, perhaps even needing to reshape whole aspects of your plot or characters—a task that will definitely take more than a single day to complete. Trying to cram all that work into just a few hours simply isn't realistic, and it's also not fair.

Ultimately, what this really comes down to is the point of this challenge.

At its core, this ten day challenge isn't here to rush you, but to guide you. It would be wrong of me to push you to complete all of your rewrites in a single day if I wasn't confident that was possible, regardless of the state of your first draft. While I can help you analyze your story and understand its flaws, putting your edits into practice is something only you can do. Because of that, this First Rest is here to act as the threshold between your first and second draft, and it won't be the only threshold you find in this challenge either. There will be a second one before we're through, along with a few smaller opportunities for rest if you need it.

However, this isn't an invitation to let yourself drag out the editing process unnecessarily. Rewriting is a difficult part of editing, but it's also completely doable so long as you remain focused and goal-oriented—just like every other challenge in this series. The only difference is that, since I can't set goals for you during this rest, you'll need to set some of your own.

Fortunately, even though I can't guide you through the specific rewrites you'll be facing, that doesn't mean I don't have some tips and tricks to share!

Making the First Rest Easier

First things first—we need to set some goals.

Before you dive into the First Rest, pull out your calendar and consider your writing schedule. At a minimum, try to commit to tackling at least one or two items from your game plan each day, adding extra time for more intense edits and less time for minor ones. Build in some backup days for when life gets in the way, but don't be afraid to be ambitious with your goals. Then, hold yourself to this schedule, the same way you'd hold yourself to a doctor's appointment or an important class. Alternatively, if your game plan is short, try blocking out a few days in a row and tackling your entire manuscript at once. Whatever makes the most sense with your writing style will work here.

Of course, this First Rest isn't only challenging because of scheduling. You'll also need to understand the purpose of the First Rest, which is to tackle the big-picture problems you've identified over the last four days. What that *doesn't* mean is "get sucked into obsessively editing your prose," or even "spend hours tweaking your dialog until it's perfect."

As tempting as it may be to get sidetracked fixing anything and everything in your draft, you need to do your best to focus on the issues with your plot, characters, worldbuilding, pacing, and point of view that you've identified in your game plan. Not only have you already put tons of brain power towards fixing these flaws, but they'll also form the foundation you'll need to handle the smaller edits that'll come later. Think of it this way—there's no point perfecting your prose only to rewrite it when you realize a scene doesn't work within your newly edited plot. If you're worried you might forget something important, take a few notes so you can revisit it later, and then continue forward.

In a similar vein, there's another habit you'll want to put into practice during the First Rest—ruthless editing.

You see, it's easy to gloss over the issues in your draft that are the hardest or most painful to fix. Cutting an otherwise likable character who no longer serves a role in your story is never fun, and many writers put this off as long as possible to avoid the stress it causes. However, you need to be ruthless when editing your novel, especially when tackling these big-picture edits. The changes you make here will have a massive impact on your final story, and could make or break its success far more than most of the smaller changes you'll work on later in the challenge.

Essentially, no matter how good a character is in isolation or how much you like a scene on its own, you have to focus on your story as a whole.

As hard as this can be, remember that your goal is to be an objective observer. Don't avoid fixing your story's flaws, because the more you kick the can down the road, the more difficult and frustrating your job will become later on.

If you still find yourself holding on to elements of your story against its best interest, consider making a copy of the scene or character you're about to change so you can edit your draft without worry. Better yet, keep an original copy of your first draft for safekeeping! This way, it'll always be there if you change your mind, giving you the mental space to continue editing without worrying about "losing" your story.

Additionally, as you work on your rewrites, you'll also need to stay organized. The game plan you created yesterday will play a big part in that, but your reverse outline will have an equally important role to play. Don't hesitate to reference your reverse outline heavily while editing your novel, rather than hunting through your entire manuscript without a guide. You can even use your reverse outline to test major changes before you make them. For example, if you need to change the order of a few scenes in your novel, reorganize them using your reverse outline first. This way you can experiment with different scenarios *before* committing any changes to your manuscript itself—which will save you a ton of time in the long run.

Alongside using your reverse outline to keep yourself organized in the present, you also want to set yourself up for success in the future. Fortunately, this is fairly simple—all you need to do is mark any problem scenes you find in your story. These could be scenes that are too slow or fast, feel incomplete, are confusing, or just seem wrong, even if you aren't sure why.

Of course, there's no need to worry about fixing these problem scenes just yet. After all, your to-do list should be focused on the big-picture problems in your story— structure, characters, pacing, et cetera. Without creating this strong foundation, it'll be almost impossible to completely remedy the problems with your scenes. So long as they're serving their role within your plot, your characters' arcs, your worldbuilding, and your pacing, leave them alone for now. We'll be shifting all of our focus to your individual scenes once the First Rest is over, and your list of problem scenes will be our first order of business.

Finally, there's one last bit of future-proofing you'll want to do throughout the First Rest.

You see, for as useful as your reverse outline is, it does require a bit of upkeep on your part. Whenever you make a revision to your draft or check an item off your to-do list, you'll need to make a record of that change in your outline as well. Without this, your reverse outline will quickly become out of date, no longer being useful for the rest of the challenge—which is the opposite of what you want.

Fortunately, this is pretty simple to keep up with. Just write a short description of what you've changed beside the appropriate scene in your timeline or character in your character sheet. This is also a great time to skim through your outline and ensure the change you made in one part of your story won't have unexpected ripple effects elsewhere. After all, it's always better to be thorough the first time, rather than realize your mistake when it's almost too late!

Other than putting these tips into practice, the First Rest is really just about hard work and patience. No matter how long your game plan is or how intense your rewrites get, always remember that you have a plan in place. Stay focused, stay calm, and keep moving forward.

Before you know it, you'll be done.

The Goals of the First Rest

As you approach the end of the First Rest, whether that's in a few days or a few weeks, you'll face one final question—how do you know when it's time to move on?

Accepting that your big-picture editing is complete can be an intimidating thing. Not only does that mean it's time to move on to the next stage of the process, but it also means you'll have new things to deal with and more flaws to face. Perhaps most difficult of all, it means you have to let go of your perfectionism.

While I've talked a lot about how damaging perfectionism can be throughout this series, that doesn't make it any easier to overcome. There's a lot of emotions attached to this feeling and accepting that many of those emotions are illogical is a difficult process. However, I want to assure you —your novel doesn't have to be perfect.

As much as editing is about perfecting and polishing your novel, nothing is ever truly perfect—and as a writer, you'll see your story's imperfections more clearly than most. Eventually, you'll have to accept those flaws and celebrate the strengths your story has, especially if you dream of one day seeing your finished novel on the shelf.

Of course, we still have nearly half of this challenge ahead of us, meaning there's plenty of time for you to keep honing and improving your story. Ultimately, the best way to know when your First Rest is complete comes from your game plan. Once you've crossed all the items off your to-do list, it's time to move on, perfect story or not. There are tons of exciting things to look forward to come Day Five, so I'll see you there very soon.

When you return we'll shift to your scenes and chapters, but for now, here are your goals for the First Rest:

1. Address all of the big-picture edits you listed in your game plan on Day Four.

2. Mark any problem scenes you come across while completing your big-picture revisions.
3. Update your reverse outline with any changes you make while editing.
4. Review your reverse outline one final time to ensure your rewrites didn't create any unexpected problems in your story.

On to Day Five!

7

DAY FIVE: CONFRONTING YOUR SCENES

W hen most people think of the editing process, they think of it in terms of drafts: first drafts, second drafts, third, and maybe even fourth drafts. However, a lot of the time, writers aren't really sure what the difference is between those drafts. Sure, the first draft is easy—it's your story in its roughest form, with no editing completed. But what exactly marks your second draft, or your third?

What's the difference?

Well, a lot of it comes down to the level of editing you've completed. Days One through Four of this challenge were all about working up to your second draft, or finishing your big-picture edits. This was about story structure, characters, worldbuilding, and your novel as a whole.

Now that you're moving into Day Five, you'll have officially finished those big-picture edits and your manuscript will be what most people would consider a second draft. Your core story is strong, and you finally have the foundation you need to begin polishing the beat by beat details of your novel. This will be your mid-level editing, encompassing your individual scenes, the transitions between them, and your novel's chapters—essentially, the smaller, still structural problems you no doubt noticed while revising your draft during the First Rest.

Of course, we won't tackle all of that at once.

Before we can dig into things like transitions or chapters, we need to make sure your story is compelling every step of the way, starting with your scenes. By the end of today, you'll be halfway to a finished novel, so welcome back! Lets get right into things.

The Requirements of a Scene

Now that you've finished your big-picture editing, your novel should be in a much better place than it was when we started. However, you'll probably still have some smaller elements of your story that need attention—specifically your scenes.

As you worked through your game plan during the First Rest, you probably noticed some scenes that just didn't work, even if you weren't sure why at the time. Fortunately, today is when we'll dive in and start putting those problem scenes back on track.

To get started, open up your reverse outline and flip to your scene timeline. Find any of the scenes you marked as problem scenes earlier on and transfer their names and details to a blank page in your reverse outline. Label this page accordingly, so you won't get it confused with your scene timeline down the road. Though that might seem impossible, trust me—it happens! This dedicated page will help keep you organized as we go, and will give you a better idea of how many scenes need substantial work.

Of course, it's entirely possible you missed some problem scenes while revising your first draft. To account for this, we're going to run a quick test before we dive into analyzing these scenes.

First up, to catch any problem scenes you may have missed, scan through your scene timeline and ask yourself these questions for each scene:

- Does my protagonist have a clear goal?
- Do they begin the scene in a different emotional or mental place than they end it?

The first of these two questions is pretty self-explanatory. Every scene needs a clear goal, both to drive your cast forward and to give that scene a purpose within your larger story. The second question, however, can be more confusing.

Essentially, what you're trying to identify is the emotional arc of the scene. Just like your novel has an emotional arc, your scenes should as well, with your protagonist ending in a different emotional state than they began. This could mean they discovered new information that changed their perspective or plans, or it could mean they've gained or lost something important. Whatever that change is—either positive or negative—every scene should have one. If they don't, that's a big red flag that that scene has problems.

So, using these two questions, mark any scenes that lack an emotional arc or a clear goal and add them to your list of problem scenes. These are the scenes you'll want to sort out before moving on from today's goals.

Fortunately, you'll likely find that you can fix most of these problem scenes with minimal work. Often it's just a simple case of one or two missing pieces that throw a scene out of balance, and this can usually be remedied quickly. Now, with all of your problem scenes in one place, we can start figuring out what these missing pieces are for each of them.

We'll be doing this two different ways.

For starters, we'll go over the most common issues scenes face, hopefully knocking out the majority of the problem scenes on your list. In all likelihood, this means that most of your scenes won't require major rewrites, which should come as a big relief! For those that you can't fix through easier methods, we'll bring in some more intensive tools—specifically scene mapping, which is similar to the story mapping you did back on Day Four.

Your first order of business when assessing your scenes should be to check whether or not they work within the guidelines of scene structure, so let's start there.

Ninety-nine percent of the scenes you write should follow scene structure to some extent. It's this structure that provides the basic framework for each scene, ensuring it not only impacts your plot, but your characters too. This means the scene is pulling double-duty, and that your story is balancing its two most important elements—overall, a win-win all around.

Since it's been a little while since we talked about scene structure, let's quickly recap some of the basics. For starters, a scene acts like its own miniature story complete with its own structure, the same as your novel. This structure is divided into six basic parts:

- **Goal:** Your characters are pursuing a goal.
- **Challenge:** They face various conflicts while trying to reach that goal.
- **Outcome:** There's an outcome, either positive or negative.
- **Reaction:** Your characters react to that outcome.
- **Reflection:** They consider their options going forward.
- **Decision (New Goal):** They make a decision, forming a new goal and beginning the cycle again.

These six parts are also split into two phases: Action and Reaction. The Action phase encompasses Goal, Challenge, and Outcome, and is focused on your characters pursuing their goals and getting into trouble.

From there we move into the Reaction phase, which is all about your cast making new plans and reflecting on their experiences thus far, making it a hugely important phase for character development. This phase encompasses Reaction, Reflection, and Decision, and can be anywhere from a sentence to an entire monologue. The Reaction phase is also when your characters decide on their next goal, which will begin the following scene. It's this goal that creates the link connecting all of your scenes together, creating a consistent thread of goals tying together your whole story.

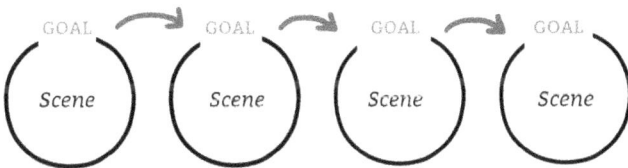

This is the basic structure your scenes should follow, and it's not unusual for writers to fix most of their problem scenes simply by making them fit within this structure.

Ask yourself—are any of your problem scenes missing one of these six parts, or are any of them particularly weak?

If you find any scenes where this is the problem, take a few notes on what specific aspects need to be repaired and how you plan to fix them. Of course, it's entirely possible some of your problem scenes have other issues, or that the ones with weak structures also have additional problems to address—which is where the next layer of this process comes in.

Reviewing your problem scenes again, make sure each scene fulfills these requirements:

- Your protagonist *must* have a goal.
- Your other core characters should also have goals of their own whenever they're present.
- Every scene should impact your story's core conflict.
- The scene should challenge your protagonist.
- Scenes should end in a different place than they began, for instance, by introducing new developments, information, allies, challenges, or emotions.
- Each scene should focus primarily on a single character's goal, even if other characters' goals are present.
- Nothing happens in isolation—the events of one scene should affect the events of later scenes.
- Scenes should be distinct, meaning they should introduce new elements, locations, characters, conflicts, or developments.

If you find a scene that fails to fulfill any of these eight requirements, write down what the problem is and any ideas you have for fixing it.

Sometimes this will be fairly easy, and it won't take long to figure out what you need to do to strengthen these scenes. However, others won't be so simple. If you're at a loss for how to remedy any of your problem scenes, here are a few quick fixes that could have a big impact:

- Change the location, add new elements, or introduce a new challenge to the scene.
- Add/remove a character to introduce a new dynamic between the members of your cast.
- Think beyond your protagonist—how will your other characters' personal goals affect their behavior and experiences in that scene?
- Consider your protagonist's character arc. How you can challenge their flaw or push them to grow?

Ideally, once you've experimented with these fixes and brainstormed ways to remedy your problem scenes, you'll find that scene mapping isn't necessary for the bulk of them. Again, if your scenes are following scene structure and your story is strong as a whole, most of your scenes should be in a good place. For any you know how to fix, go ahead and make those changes in both your reverse outline and your draft.

Unfortunately, there always seems to be at least one or two scenes that just don't work, often for no explainable reason. So, for any lingering scenes you can't seem to fix, now is the time to bring out the highlighters—it's scene mapping time!

Tackling Your Problem Scenes

At this point, scene mapping will probably feel pretty familiar—after all, you went through a very similar process when mapping your story back on Day Four. Still, there will be some differences, and because of that this is usually a process I reserve for only the most problematic scenes.

While you could do this for every scene in your novel, there are a lot of variables to consider, and you want to take your time to ensure you interpret your results correctly. This is because, at its core, scene mapping is about analyzing the pacing of your scenes. However, with a bit of careful consideration you'll quickly find that it can tell you about far more than just pacing, making it a great second line of defense after reviewing the questions we just covered. We're only human, and it's easy to miss problems the first time around. Personally, I've found everything from scenes without a clear conflict to entirely missing Reaction phases through scene mapping.

To start this process for your own problem scenes, first choose a handful of colored markers, highlighters, pens, or pencils. Then create a key for these five things:

- Action
- Description
- Exposition
- Dialog
- Reflection

Here's a quick example of what each of these will look like within your scenes:

- **Action:** I stood up, jogging down the hill to catch Fido before he dug his way out of the dog park.
- **Description:** His fur was matted with mud and leaves, and when he looked up at me his puppy-dog eyes shone through a mask of wet dirt.
- **Exposition:** I had found Fido as a stray a few months ago, and I had adored him ever since.
- **Dialog:** "Come here boy, I think it's time for us to go home," I said, trying to be stern but struggling not to laugh at his muddy face.
- **Reflection:** I was endlessly grateful that Fido had adjusted to living with me so quickly—even though my small apartment wasn't ideal for a growing puppy, he had made himself right at home.

Note that these categories differ from the action-dominant or character-dominant designations you gave your scenes back on Day Four. Those were more about the role each scene played in your whole story, meaning that regardless of which designation you gave, you should still find a mixture of these five things in all of your scenes.

So, with your key ready to go, choose one of your remaining problem scenes and flip to where it starts in your draft.

The goal of scene mapping is to mark each paragraph in your chosen scene using the five categories above. Skimming through the scene, highlight each paragraph based on the key you created. As you go, you'll likely find that you write in blocks—you'll have one or two paragraphs that fall predominantly under action, and then a paragraph or two for dialog, exposition, or even description. Of course, some paragraphs will have a mixture of multiple categories so, just like with story mapping, pick whichever category is most dominant in that paragraph.

Once you've done this for every paragraph in your problem scene, next comes the task of interpreting those colors.

For starters, this mapping process should give you a strong sense of the pacing of your scene. With just a simple glance, you can see if a scene is predominantly action, dialog, description, exposition, or reflection, and whether there's much variation within that scene. If you find that your scene is almost entirely dominated by a single color, that's a red flag, and might explain why you marked it as a problem scene in the first place. Ideally, you want to strike a balance between all five of these categories, even though one category will probably make up the majority of your scene.

To remedy this, look for areas that are only one color and think about how you could mix in other categories. For instance, blend action into long periods of dialog, exposition, or reflection to keep the reader grounded in the setting of your story. Likewise, if your problem scene is nothing but action, set aside some time for description and reflection, even if it's just a paragraph or two to even things out.

Ultimately, without this healthy balance, your scene is likely missing one of the fundamental components we talked about earlier on. This goes for all five categories—if only one type of paragraph is dominating your entire scene, you likely have a bigger flaw lurking underneath:

- **Only Action:** The scene may lack a Reaction phase, or have a very weak Reaction phase.
- **Only Description:** The scene may lack a strong conflict or driving goal.
- **Only Exposition:** The scene may be extraneous, without a goal or conflict driving it forward.
- **Only Dialog:** The scene may be disorienting for your

reader without something to ground them in a specific time and place.
- **Only Reflection:** The scene may lack an Action phase, or may have a very weak Action phase.

As an example, this is a common problem in scenes where characters are having a long conversation with little going on around them—the author will become so absorbed in the scene's dialog that they'll forget to tell us what's happening during that conversation. When the conversation finally ends, the reader will be left to do a double take, struggling to remember where everything is happening and how much time has passed.

Ideally, in situations like these you want to balance the scene, mixing up long sections of dialog with a bit of description and action. Instead of marching through the characters' conversation without a break, pause for a moment to talk about one character nervously playing with their hair while speaking, or to mention how the bell above the restaurant door rings when it opens. This not only pulls the characters from their thoughts and potentially adds some extra tension, but it also reminds your reader where they are.

In a similar vein, when describing settings or delivering exposition, you need to balance things out with moments of action or reflection to remind your reader that they're reading a novel—not a historical account or a newspaper article. The only exception to this is for extended flashbacks, where all the action and reflection should occur in the flashback itself, not in the present.

Of course, while scene mapping is simple to me thanks to lots of practice, interpreting your own results may not be as intuitive for you. As is the case with so many parts of the editing process, the fact that you're so familiar with your own manuscript can make it hard to see your scenes' pacing objectively.

Fortunately, there is a trick that makes this easier!

To help you gain a better perspective, try pulling out another book in your novel's genre, preferably one that inspires you or that you admire. Then flip to a scene in a similar part of that story as the one you're working on and map it. This is very easy to do on Kindles and other e-readers, since you can highlight passages right in the app, but you can also do this in a paperback using sticky tabs or washi tape.

Once you've finished mapping the scene, look back through to see how it balances each of the five different categories. This should give you a good idea, not only of how to interpret your own results, but also of what other books in your genre do when pacing their scenes.

Finally, as you map your remaining problem scenes, take notes on the issues you find.

Are there huge blocks of exposition or action? Alternatively, if there's no action at all, is your scene missing a compelling conflict? Take notes on all these things and brainstorm the best ways to fix the problems you find. Sometimes this is as simple as adding a few paragraphs to supplement the categories you're missing, while other scenes may need significant restructuring.

Whatever changes you have to make, make sure you update your reverse outline and ensure each newly rewritten scene still works within your novel as a whole—just like you did during the First Rest.

THE TEN DAY EDIT

An Optional Rest

Of course, there are multiple ways to approach fixing your problem scenes.

Personally, I prefer reviewing, mapping, and then fixing each scene as I go, to keep my thoughts focused on one thing at a time. However, you can also map all of your problem scenes and then carve out a large chunk of time to fix them, similar to what we did with the First Rest—and this is where your first optional rest comes in.

Ideally, you'll find that you don't have that many problem scenes to deal with in the first place, thanks to the analysis and editing we did at the start of this challenge. Even among the problem scenes you *do* find, most should be fixable with minor changes and revisions—very few scenes need to be completely rewritten at this stage, at least most of the time.

Still, it is possible you'll have a few scenes that need major fixes, and just like I didn't want to rush you during the First Rest, I don't want to rush you here. If you have to take a few extra days to finish reworking your problem scenes, know that you have my blessing. However, the same thing I said for the First Rest applies here too—only do this if you truly need to. The point of this challenge is to stay focused and moving forward, rather than letting the editing process drag out indefinitely. If you choose to take advantage of this optional rest, make sure you're still making progress throughout.

Fortunately, most of the time today's goals go by fairly smoothly. Even if you have to take an extra day to wrap up your last few problem scenes, that's ok!

Just like with the First Rest, you've got a plan and you know what you need to do—now it's just a matter of doing it.

The Goals of Day Five

Day Five is one of those weird days in this challenge where it can either go really well, or really poorly. Whereas I usually know which days will be the easiest or the hardest before I even get started, Day Five always eludes me, no matter how many times I complete this process. Still, whether or not you struggle today, the tips and tricks in this chapter should help you overcome any hurdles you might face.

By the end of today, your scenes and their pacing should be strong, but they won't be complete just yet. That's because Day Six is when we'll finally connect your scenes as a unified whole, and when your manuscript will start looking like a real, finished novel. I hope you're excited!

Tomorrow we'll turn your draft into a page-turner, but for now, here are the goals you've completed for Day Five:

1. Identify any problem scenes in your draft, either based on notes you took during the First Rest or through a series of questions.
2. Separate these problem scenes from the rest of your scene timeline.
3. Revise these problem scenes until they fulfill all the requirements of a scene.
4. For any scenes you can't seem to fix, map their pacing to identify what's wrong.

On to Day Six!

8

DAY SIX: WHAT CREATES A PAGE-TURNER?

I t's no secret that readers live for page-turning novels, for the thrill of a story that grips their attention and doesn't let go even long after they've put the book down. Likewise, many authors dream of writing a novel that could achieve this coveted status—but what they don't realize is that there's no magic to creating a page-turner. In fact, many page-turning novels aren't particularly groundbreaking in either their storytelling or their writing.

Instead, what creates a page-turner is all about pacing.

As we've talked about often throughout this challenge, pacing is one of the fundamental elements of your novel. Not only does it shape your reader's experience, but it keeps them invested in what's happening on the page—and on the next page, and the next, and the next. When it comes to pacing, even an average story with excellent pacing can succeed over a brilliant one with horrible pacing, simply because pacing affects so many layers of your story.

For instance, there's the big-picture pacing we talked about earlier in this challenge, which shapes how your story plays out across your entire novel. This pacing determines how you balance your conflict and characters, and how you increase the tension of your plot as you approach the finale. Similarly, you also have the pacing of your scenes, though these operate on a slightly smaller scale. Finally, completing the trio is the pacing we'll be talking about today—the pacing of your chapters.

Ask yourself—what is the main unit of a novel in the eyes of readers? While you might see your story in terms of acts or scenes, a reader will understand it in terms of chapters, meaning the way you structure those chapters will have a big impact on how they experience your story.

Of course, this is about more than just slapping some chapter breaks on your manuscript and calling it a day. Just like everything else we've done throughout this challenge, there's a method to the madness. Fortunately, your pacing doesn't have much farther to go. With just a bit more work on your scenes and chapters, your novel will be that much closer to page-turner status, and you'll be that much more ready to share it with the world!

Transitioning Between Scenes

There are so many layers involved in good storytelling. On the one hand, your story's structure and characters shape the tale you're telling on a grand scale, while things like writing style lend a unique voice to your novel one word at a time.

Somewhere in the middle of these two extremes is pacing.

Like I mentioned previously, pacing impacts not only your overarching story, but also the beat-by-beat experience of your readers. A balanced pace keeps your novel intriguing and interesting, sure, but it also ensures your readers never find themselves lost in your story.

It's this second role of pacing that we're going to focus on today, starting with your scene transitions.

Scene transitions are the brief periods between when one scene ends and another begins, orienting your reader in both the setting and time of the new scene. Often these are only a sentence or two, but they can occasionally stretch out to full paragraphs. This provides important context to your reader, letting them know who is present in the new scene, where it's happening, and how much time has passed. Without these scene transitions, readers are left confused and frustrated, grinding the pacing of your story to a halt as your reader struggles to figure out what they've missed.

Fortunately, at this point in the challenge your scenes should be in their final form, meaning you can finally turn your attention to the transitions between them. Best of all, thanks to the scene structure you put in place yesterday your scenes should already have at least some logical connection—connections you can build on today.

To start, lets establish some basic rules for scene transitions. First and foremost, your job when transitioning between scenes is to guide your reader from one scene to the next. Even though readers will understand that your story is shifting to a new scene, you still need to provide the right details so they can stay immersed in your story. You never, *ever* want your readers to ask, "Wait, what's happening?"

This is a lot like when you first introduce a new setting—not only do you tell the reader who is present, but you also provide important details about that location and where it exists in relation to your larger story. If you're having trouble visualizing this, think of the sweeping landscape shots from any of the three *The Lord of the Rings* movies. While these are beautiful in their own right, they serve an even more important role, showing us the distances these characters are traveling and giving us a sense that time is passing as we move from scene to scene. This can be done on a smaller scale too, often with just a brief line of exposition.

Specifically, when reviewing your scene transitions, make sure they include:

- Who is present
- What is happening
- How much time has passed
- Where the characters are
- A hint at your protagonist's goal for the scene
- Any other critical information the reader will need

Of course, there's no need to open every scene by saying, "It's been two days, and I've gone to work, come home, slept, showered, and gone to work again." Instead, you want to strike a balance between providing important context, and finishing your scene transitions quickly. Usually, you'll only need a sentence or two to get your reader up to speed, while major jumps in time or location might require a full paragraph. Most of the time, tedious details beyond the basics we listed above aren't necessary—so long as your reader will understand them through context.

For example, in a detective drama the writer often won't show the lab work being done between scenes, because they can imply it was completed off screen when the cast gathers to inspect that evidence later on. The reader will still be able to follow what's happening, because there are enough context clues to keep them in the loop.

To see this at work in a novel similar to yours, pull out the book you mapped yesterday and return to the scene you analyzed. Specifically, consider the beginning and end of that scene. How did it handle the transition from the previous scene to the next? What did it do to keep you oriented as a reader? You'll likely find that, no matter what scene you look at, each is framed by a quick bit of exposition or description —exactly the scene transitions we're working on today.

So, flip through your own manuscript, paying special attention to the beginning and end of your scenes. Hopefully, you'll find that you included a lot of these scene transitions instinctively—most of us are used to them thanks to other novels we've read, and we subconsciously add them to our own stories as a result. If you find any scenes that lack these transitions, think about the critical information your reader will need to stay oriented. Then incorporate those details into the start of that scene.

Of course, it's not always easy to balance both trusting your readers and providing enough information.

If you're having trouble with the transitions between any of your scenes, focus on the first two paragraphs after the scene begins. Even if that scene doesn't immediately provide all the details we discussed, does it still cover those five basic elements within the first two paragraphs? Some scenes open with dialog or lone sentences, so which paragraphs count as your first two is largely up to your own judgment. So long as the scene introduces these details as soon as is reasonable, you can usually trust your readers to keep up.

However, if those details—who is present, how much time has passed, and where we are—stretch beyond your first two paragraphs, pause and ask yourself why. There are certainly instances when this is necessary, such as when long periods of time have passed and your readers need a more in-depth recap, which is when that "any other critical information" clause really comes into play. Still, this is not the norm.

At the end of the day, if you can justify it, then don't worry. Just remember that, at least most of the time, two paragraphs is enough. Ultimately, the goal here is to ensure your readers never have to put your book down or flip back a page to figure out what's happening, potentially giving up on your story along the way.

The Basics of Chapter Structure

With your scenes officially complete, you now have a long, seamless manuscript sitting on your desk—meaning the only things left to tackle are your chapters.

Until now you shouldn't have had any chapters marked in your manuscript, at least if you followed my instructions back on Day Zero, and this was for a few reasons.

For one, it hopefully made it much easier to revise large sections of your story without the added worry of disturbing your chapters. It should also have made it easier for you to identify the beginning and end of your scenes, since chapter breaks can muddy the waters at that stage. Finally, it means you can now create chapters with the best understanding of your story possible, along with a bit of chapter structure to guide you!

You see, chapters are a powerful tool for shaping your reader's experience, but they're often sorely misunderstood.

While there's a lot of nuance to how chapters work, many writers mistakenly think they have to rely on cliffhangers and other tricks to keep their readers engaged. In reality, you shouldn't string readers along. Strong chapter structure will naturally make your story more compelling and engaging, because well-structured chapters push your reader through your story like a funnel, all while keeping them grounded in what's happening.

This is why scene and chapter structure form the mid-level stage of this editing process. Not only do they shape the moment-to-moment beats of your story, but they also decide whether or not your novel will fall into that coveted category of "page-turner."

Of course, to create your chapters, we first need to cover some basics. For starters, chapters and scenes *are not* the same thing. As we've talked about in the past, scenes are the individual units that make up your story, acting as micro stories within your larger novel. On the other hand, chapters are the logical collections of these individual scenes.

Your scenes are about how you tell your story, while your chapters are about how your readers experience that story.

This means that chapters can contain anywhere from one to multiple scenes—or even just half a scene. In fact, a chapter could contain tons of odd combinations like two and a half or four and a half scenes, so long as those scenes fit within what is called your chapter funnel. This chapter funnel is the basic, four-level structure your chapters should follow:

- **Level One:** The opening of the funnel introduces where your protagonist is, when, and why. At this stage, your protagonist has many options to pursue.
- **Level Two:** Next your protagonist sets their eyes on

a goal, beginning to narrow that funnel.

- **Level Three:** Your protagonist then faces conflicts and challenges while pursuing their chapter goal, pushing them towards the culmination of that goal at the end of the chapter.
- **Level Four:** Eventually the funnel reaches its point, where your protagonist faces the primary conflict of that chapter and either succeeds or fails.

From there, your next chapter returns to Level One, or the widest part of the funnel. There your protagonist is in a new state thanks to the results of the previous chapter, complete with a new goal and plenty of options to pursue—just like the Decision stage of a scene.

THE BASIC CHAPTER FUNNEL

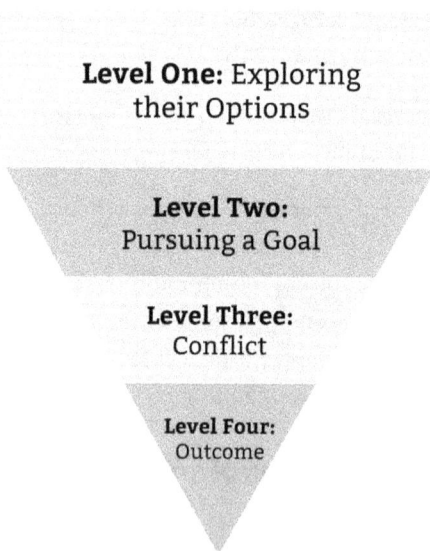

Level One: Exploring
their Options

Level Two:
Pursuing a Goal

Level Three:
Conflict

Level Four:
Outcome

By this point, I imagine this structure feels pretty familiar. After all, the core idea of any structure is to present a cohesive beginning, middle and end, tying it all together with a single conflict—chapters are no different. However, unlike your novel's core conflict, your chapter conflicts will usually be more subtle.

Every chapter doesn't need to end with a climactic battle or world-ending stakes, and the various conflicts within your individual chapters *will* seem small when compared to the core conflict of your entire novel.

Instead, what you need is a clear goal connecting every scene in each chapter. From there, you can slowly increase the tension and narrow your protagonist's options until they reach the conclusion of that goal. This will force your reader to question whether your protagonist will succeed, driving them to keep reading as they become more and more invested in your protagonist's journey. Even this should feel familiar—it's the core idea behind the Dramatic Question we talked about all the way back on Day One!

Of course, there are exceptions to every rule, and for chapters that comes in the form of cliffhangers. This is where the chapter cuts off right at the end of the funnel, before it reaches its culmination. The next chapter then wraps up what the previous one started, essentially splitting your chapter funnel between two chapters.

This means that, while some view cliffhangers as a stylistic choice based only on personal preference or genre, they do have some foundation in chapter structure. So long as they're done well and used sparingly, cliffhangers can help add tension to major scenes. However, when used too often it can quickly feel like you're baiting your reader, rather than giving them the satisfaction of a proper culmination.

THE CLIFFHANGER CHAPTER FUNNEL

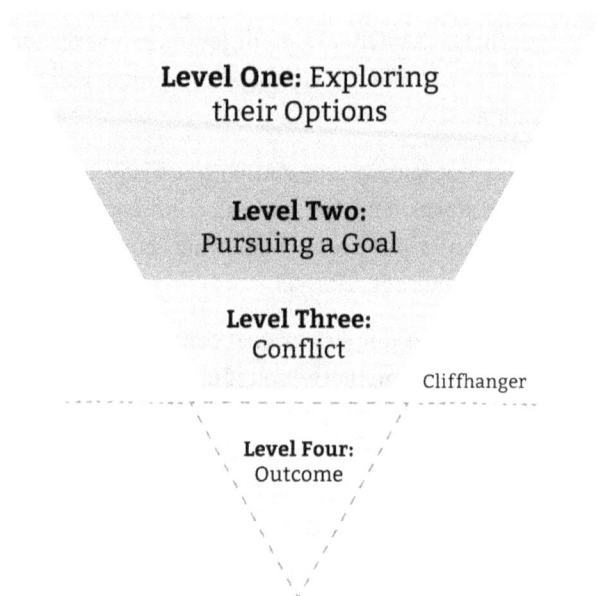

Level One: Exploring
their Options

Level Two:
Pursuing a Goal

Level Three:
Conflict

Cliffhanger

Level Four:
Outcome

Really, the best metric for when a cliffhanger is appropriate is whether the end of that chapter funnel is large enough to encompass an entire chapter on its own. This will usually happen around your major plot points, simply because there is so much material to cover and conflict to explore.

Otherwise, think carefully before you create a cliffhanger— while you can certainly add one, you always want to do so for the right reasons!

Creating Chapters of Your Own

With the basics of chapter structure out of the way, you can begin applying this structure to your own novel. Of course, figuring out where to start in your one hundred plus page manuscript can be daunting, which is where your reverse outlines comes to the rescue—again!

Since chapters are built from groups of interconnected scenes, your scene timeline is the perfect place to create your chapters. This will allow you to experiment with your chapter breaks until you land on a structure that works for your story, all without having to touch your manuscript.

To get started, first think about how the different scenes in your novel connect. What common threads or goals run through your scenes? Even though each scene in your novel will have its own individual goal, the goals of some scenes will actually be closely linked. These scenes then become logical candidates for being combined into a single chapter.

For example, here are three scenes goals that would fit well together as a chapter:

- **First Scene Goal:** Reach the military complex.
- **Second Scene Goal:** Create a plan.
- **Third Scene Goal:** Sneak past the guards.

As you can see, all of these scenes are connected by the larger goal of getting into the military complex. Not only does this make them strong candidates for a chapter, but they'll also flow nicely into following chapter goals, such as helping the captives escape. In this way, your chapters function similarly to your scenes—each one has its own goal that then connects to the next.

Looking through your scene timeline, think about how your various scenes connect. Some will jump out at you as strong candidates immediately, so mark those in your timeline and write their shared chapter goal beneath them. Then, consider how they work together to create the funnel effect we discussed earlier—the first scene in the chapter should offer more flexibility for your protagonist, while the final one should end with a culmination of the chapter's goal. Of course, some chapters will only have one scene, simply because that individual scene is climactic enough to warrant its own chapter. This is usually the case when you're dealing with major plot points, since these scenes will naturally have a larger impact on your story.

For instance, playing off our rescue mission example from above, a single chapter within that story might focus entirely on an interrogation scene after the protagonist is caught helping the captives escape. This would work as a standalone chapter because, at least in this hypothetical scenario, they would face the antagonist, confront their own flaws, and eventually break free after making an important decision. Basically, the Midpoint!

Of course, while structuring your chapters, you'll want to consider a few things beyond the basic chapter funnel we've discussed.

For starters, try to avoid chapters that all have the same emotional impact one after another. Regardless of what that emotional impact is, this can cause your story to feel monotonous and emotionally flat. To avoid this, write the primary emotion of each chapter alongside its goal, ensuring you're mixing things up and keeping your story fresh. While focusing on one primary emotion for multiple chapters is ok, consider exploring different dimensions of that emotion. For example, instead of every chapter centering on happiness, have some explore hope, humor, or anticipation. Fortunately, this shouldn't require much rewriting on your part, and will instead be about how you group your scenes.

Additionally, different genres will have different conventions when it comes to chapters, and these are worth paying attention to. Some genres work best with lots of short, single scene chapters—such as thrillers—while others lean towards longer multi-scene ones.

Just like many aspects of the editing process, this is another place where researching popular books in your genre can be very valuable. Not only can it clue you into what your future readers are expecting, but it might even give you ideas for how to combine some of your trickier scenes.

Finally, more than anything else, chapters are about shaping how your reader experiences your story.

When creating your chapters, you need to think about what you want your reader's experience to be like. Is your story best in short bursts, perfect for readers on vacation or riding the subway? Alternatively, is your novel better read in large chunks, letting your reader sink into your world and the many adventures it has to offer?

While it's always good to mix things up and include chapters of both sizes, try to put yourself in your readers shoes—what type of chapter will give them the best reading experience possible?

By the end of this process, you'll want your scene timeline to be fully organized by chapter, with each chapter's goal written in the margins. Once you're happy with what you've created, transfer these chapter breaks to your manuscript itself. If you plan to title your chapters, do so now—if not, you're officially done with Day Six!

The Goals of Day Six

As today comes to a close, you've officially completed your mid-level editing. That's a big milestone in its own right, but it also comes with an added benefit—you can now look through your manuscript and see your final novel taking shape. The end of Day Six is incredibly gratifying as a result, simply because of how exciting it is to have what looks like a finished novel on your hands!

Of course, there's still plenty to do, from gathering feedback to putting the final coat of polish on your prose. However, all of that can wait.

For now, I hope you'll take some time to curl up in a comfy chair, grab a friend, and relish in how amazing it is that this story of yours has come so far. Forgive me for waxing poetic, but the sight of chapters after so long without them is like finding water in a creative desert—enjoy it!

Tomorrow we'll share your story with the world, but for now, here are the goals you've completed for Day Six:

1. Review the transitions between your scenes, ensuring they keep readers oriented within the time and place of your story.
2. Returning to your scene timeline, organize your scenes based on common goals.
3. Turn these groupings into chapters, making sure they create a funnel effect.
4. Add these final chapter breaks and their titles to your manuscript.

On to the Second Rest!

9

THE SECOND REST

There are few things more painful as a writer than sharing our works in progress, only to be met with disinterest. This is a crushing experience, and many would rather have their novels torn to shreds or outright reviled than ignored—at least then people are paying attention.

On the other end of this spectrum, perhaps the fastest way to inflate a writer's ego is to lavish their first draft with praise. Many of us have someone in our lives who will always tell us our storytelling is perfect, no matter how flawed it may be. They mean well—truly, they do—but just like those ignoring our stories, they don't realize the harm they're actually causing.

You see, your early drafts are by far the most vulnerable stage of your novel's life. Not only are you struggling to remain objective about your writing, but your story itself is in flux, and this means almost anything can push you off course. Cruelty will quickly blot out the good in your novel, while kindness will blind you to the bad. It's for this reason that I've yet to encourage you to share your draft throughout this editing challenge. While getting feedback on your story is important for your novel's success, knowing when to avoid sharing is just as valuable.

However, there is a time for feedback, and that time is now.

Unlike your first or even second drafts, your story is now in a solid place, your scenes are strong, and your pacing is polished—meaning it's finally safe to share your novel with other people. So, just like we paused this challenge for the First Rest, we'll be pausing it again today.

This Second Rest is largely meant as a courtesy to your readers, giving them the time to process your story and gather their thoughts, but it's also here for you to take a much-deserved break. You've been working incredibly hard the last few weeks, and your brain likely needs some time to recharge. Of course, knowing which readers to approach and how to handle their feedback will go a long way in making this a more pleasant experience. You'll likely have a lot of information to sift through when we return on Day Seven, so before this rest can begin, we have some prep work to do.

The Value of Feedback

No matter how much I go on and on about the importance of gathering feedback, you may still be thinking—does it *really* matter?

Is getting other people's opinions really that important?

Well, for starters, outside feedback is the truest way to gain an objective view of your story. Unlike when you're editing your own writing, the people who review your draft will approach your story with fresh eyes, allowing them to see things more clearly in the process. Not only that, but their feedback will act as a window into your future readers' minds. Even the most basic feedback can give you an idea of whether your core story is working, while some readers will offer more specific thoughts and critiques.

Of course, there are different groups you can turn to for feedback, and each one will offer different levels of expertise. Specifically, there are four you'll need to know about:

———

Beta Readers:

Beta readers are the closest any of these groups will come to your target readership, and will provide the most general feedback of the four. Ideally, beta readers should already be fans and frequent readers of the genre you're writing in. This allows them to truly experience your story for what it is, letting you know how well future readers will respond to your novel.

However, precisely because of this more general feedback, beta readers are best worked with en masse.

To really get the most out of beta readers, you want to work with anywhere from five to fifteen at a time—though I discourage you from going much higher than fifteen, as you can quickly become overwhelmed by all of their thoughts. Rather than focusing on specific details, this large collection of feedback will help you identify common trends or consistent problems in your story.

Critique Partners:

Critique partners are almost always fellow writers, or at least storytelling enthusiasts who can provide a more experienced perspective on your novel. Their feedback will be a bit more precise, and will likely include more details and usable advice than the average beta reader could offer.

Usually these are one-on-one relationships too—in exchange for providing feedback on your manuscript, you'll usually do the same for them. Because of this, finding and working with a critique partner is a great way to build relationships with other writers, while simultaneously gaining some extra editing experience for yourself!

Professional Editors:

If you want to fast-track your storytelling skills, your best option by far is to work with a professional editor. These are the experts of the writing world, and they'll be able to leverage all of their experience and wisdom to help you root out any remaining problems in your story. Of course, this does come with a higher investment on your part, as good editors aren't cheap. Still, out of all four groups you could approach for feedback, editors will offer the most targeted and useful advice of the bunch.

The Internet:

Ah yes... the internet. While many people are used to turning to the Internet for almost anything, soliciting feedback for your manuscript should not be on that list.

The internet comes with a huge variety of problems—from just a general viciousness to a lack of constructive criticism —making it anything but ideal for most writers. Despite this, some writers still love sharing their work on internet forums and online platforms, and more power to them. However, if you're not confident in your own writing skills and your ability to sort through the potentially questionable feedback you receive, I recommend looking elsewhere.

——————

These groups all have their place when gathering feedback for your novel—except maybe the internet—and it's well worth your time to work with as many as possible. Realistically, however, that may not be possible for you. Editors are a big investment, regardless of how valuable they are, and beta readers take a lot of time and energy to manage. Even critique partners require commitment and work on your part.

Unfortunately, none of these options are without their drawbacks. Knowing how to pick the right readers for your situation is important, especially if you want to get the most out of this round of feedback. A few of the things that may influence your decision are:

- What you can afford.
- How much time you can spend.
- What connections you already have.
- What kind of advice you'd find most useful.

So, to help you sort through these different options, let's look at the process involved with each of these groups and how you might go about gathering their feedback.

Picking the Right Readers

Starting at the top of our list, beta readers are almost always the cheapest option, and will usually read your manuscript for free. However, they also take a decent amount of time to both find and work with, requiring regular check-ins and detailed instruction on your part.

If you already have an established audience of some kind, whether through an author website, social media, or your newsletter, you can often reach out to these subscribers to offer an early copy of your new novel in exchange for feedback. Fans of yours will often jump at this opportunity, making it a great way to speed up the otherwise long process of finding beta readers.

Fortunately, you don't have to have an existing audience to find beta readers!

There are often local beta reading groups in major cities, and there are even online groups that specialize in specific genres. However, if you join one of these groups, expect to beta read for others as well—and make sure you say yes. If the group is doing you the favor of reviewing your novel for free, you should absolutely do the same for them.

Of course, it's important to note that not all beta readers are created equal. Beta readers are there to act as a test audience first and foremost, so you want to pick a group of people who regularly read and enjoy novels like yours—essentially, your target readers.

If you're reaching out to people who are already part of your own audience, this should be a given, so you can safely assume they're at least interested in the novels you write. However, if you're approaching an outside group of beta readers or even connections through social media, there are a few things you'll want to ask to determine whether or not they're a good fit for your story:

- What genres do they typically read?

- How many books do they read in the average year?
- Do they read for action or emotional engagement?
- How old are they, and what is their gender?

Asking what genres they read and how often are both pretty self-explanatory, since you want to pick beta readers who enjoy books similar to yours. Whether they read for action or emotion is just another easy way to get a feel for how they'll approach your novel—someone who reads purely for action probably isn't the right fit for a slow, introspective literary novel, no matter how great they are!

It's the demographic questions on this list that are by far the hardest ones, but these may or may not be super important to your situation.

If you know your novel is targeting a specific demographic, say middle-aged women, then including at least a few of those readers in your beta group is a smart move. On the other hand, if your novel is meant to appeal to a broader slice of the population, you can probably omit these entirely. Either way, always make a point to ask these questions with respect, for obvious reasons. And of course, don't be afraid to include a mix of people in your beta reading group! Even if they aren't an exact match to your target reader, they can still provide useful feedback and a unique perspective on your story that you may really appreciate.

Fortunately, if you're working with beta readers online, you can ask all these questions through either an online survey or a quick email. If you're working with a preexisting beta group, ask how they go about this process, or if they have a screening process at all. Above all, remember to be respectful and gracious. If a group doesn't have a process of any kind, but are already geared towards your target genre, then you don't really need to worry. If they don't, ask yourself if you still think they'd be a good fit for your novel—if not, thank them for their time and look for another group.

Finally, you need to know what you're getting into if you decide to work with beta readers.

Beta readers are usually avid consumers of a particular genre, but they aren't often writers themselves. This means the feedback they give you will likely be more generalized. Expect things like, "I really liked the protagonist" or "the middle of the story felt boring."

This kind of feedback is definitely valuable, because it highlights the ways your target reader will experience your story. However, it will require more time on your part to interpret the trends you find and figure out how to actually address those concerns. If you're up for that—and you probably should be, beta readers are a wonderful resource—then beta readers could be a great choice!

Long story short, when considering if beta readers are right for your story, here's the breakdown:

- Beta readers are usually free, but you want to work with at least five to get the most useful feedback.
- You can find beta readers without existing connections, though having a preexisting audience will speed up the process.
- Beta readers won't give the most detailed advice, and will usually focus more on how the story felt.

Next on our list are critique partners, what most writers would consider the middle option of the three. Critique partners are an awesome resource to have, both because they're more experienced than the average beta reader, but also because they can quickly become lifelong connections and writing friends!

While every critique partner agreement is slightly different, usually the two of you will swap manuscripts in exchange for feedback. You'll review their story and they'll do the same for you, before you both meet up to discuss your thoughts and share constructive criticism.

The real difference between this kind of reader and beta readers is that critique partners are almost always fellow writers. This means their feedback will be more in-depth, and will likely include specific areas for improvement— something along the long of "your protagonist's character arc felt weak" or "your Resolution was strong." This can save you a ton of time when compared to beta readers, since you won't have to sift through their feedback struggling to understand what the problem really is. Most of the time they'll be able to tell you exactly what they thought was wrong up front, and if not, you can often get a better idea simply by talking with them.

Of course, this is also what makes critique partners more difficult to find—these kinds of partnerships are almost always built from existing friendships.

If you don't already have writing friends to work with, you'll need to take some time to either reach out to other writers and introduce yourself or join an existing critique group. Like existing beta reader groups, you'll be expected to follow their rules and give back in some way, so plan to share your own feedback in exchange for their help

Above all, whether you work with an individual critique partner or a group, make sure they're someone you enjoy working with and can trust with your story. Ideally, critique partners will be at similar points in the writing process as well—critiquing someone else's novel is a big time commitment, so working with someone who is also taking a break to gather feedback is the perfect situation. You can both critique each other's work while you have the time to spend, before moving on to finalize your own novels. Plus, if you're at similar points in the editing process, you can share tips, tricks, and moral support too!

Ultimately, if you're considering working with a critique partner, keep these things in mind:

- Critique partners are usually free, but expect to spend a good amount of time critiquing their manuscript in return for feedback on your own.
- Finding a critique partner is much easier if you already have a circle of writing friends, though you can find local or online groups to join as well.
- Critique partners can offer more detailed feedback than beta readers, since they are writers themselves.

Last but not least, we have editors.

These are the experts of the writing world, and they'll be able to offer by far the most in-depth and useful feedback of any of the options we've explored. However, that does come with a trade off—editors are professionals, and they charge accordingly.

Even still, if you have the means to invest in one, I encourage everyone to work with an editor if they can. Not only will an editor be able to improve the novel you're currently working on by leaps and bounds, but they'll also offer advice that you can apply to every novel you write from here on out. While the investment is certainly significant, this means that working with an editor is by far the fastest way to jumpstart the quality of your storytelling.

Of course, it's important to know that there are many types of professional editors, and the one you'll want to work with will largely depend on where you are in the editing process. Specifically, there are four types you're likely to run into:

———

Developmental Editors:

These editors are there to focus on the quality of your storytelling, and will provide feedback on things like story structure, character arcs, theme, pacing, and genre. This is the first type of editor you should work with when editing your novel.

Copy Editors:

A copy editor's job is, first and foremost, to ensure that your writing is cohesive and compelling. They'll correct issues of grammar and spelling to some extent, but their real focus will be on tense, sentence structure, clarity, and style.

Line Editors:

Line editors and copy editors fulfill essentially the same role, and these terms are often used interchangeably. If you're unsure what your line or copy editor focuses on, ask them to specify what issues they'll look for in your manuscript.

Proofreaders:

Finally, proofreaders are all about polishing your finished novel. They'll correct your spelling, capitalization, grammar, and punctuation, and ensure you don't have any typos lingering in your final draft.

———

At this stage in the editing process, you'll want to find and work with a developmental editor. We'll be shifting focus to your prose soon, but for now, this round of feedback is about ensuring your story and storytelling are as strong as they can be—and hiring a developmental editor is the fastest way to do that.

Fortunately, you can find a huge variety of developmental editors with just a quick online search.

Most developmental editors specialize in specific genres, so do your research and find a few that have experience editing novels like yours. Then, look for reviews to see what other writers thought of their work, and schedule a consultation with your top choice. This will give you a chance to both talk with the editor, and to get to know each other. Above all, it'll help you decide whether or not you feel comfortable investing in that person's expertise. Definitely don't be afraid to have consultations with two or three editors until you decide who is the best fit for you and your story—this can take a bit of time, but once you find an editor you enjoy working with you'll likely come back to them again and again!

If you're planning to work with a professional editor, here's what you should keep in mind:

- Editors are an investment—you're paying for their expertise and years of experience.
- You can easily find professional editors online, or through recommendations from fellow writers and writing friends.
- A developmental editor will provide *by far* the most

detailed feedback of any group we've talked about, making them the fastest way to improve your storytelling skills.

Setting Expectations

Once you've decided what types of readers are the best fit for your manuscript, it's time to reach out to them.

Send an email to your audience or post on social media looking for beta readers. Call up a writing friend to ask about swapping manuscripts as critique partners, or look up some local critique groups and start attending. Better yet, schedule a consultation with a professional editor if you can. Ideally, you'll want to pick at least two of these groups to work with to get the best range of feedback for your novel.

From there, you'll need to set the right expectations with each group.

For starters, be clear that you've heavily edited your manuscript for plot and structure, but not for prose. This means your story is basically in its final form, but that your manuscript may still have typos, misspellings, and other similar errors—though hopefully you've weeded out at least some of these over the last few days. This also means that you aren't looking for line editing or feedback on your writing style. Instead, you want your readers to focus on the quality of your story itself, specifically things like your story's structure, characters, and pacing. This is most important when working with beta readers or critique partners, and a quick email letting them know the current state of your draft will usually be plenty for them to understand. You might also choose to share a few specific questions or notes to guide their feedback. This lets them know exactly what issues you want them to pay attention to, and can be a great way to encourage more targeted feedback.

Of course, if you're working with a developmental editor they should already be aware of most of these things, though it never hurts to let them know about any specific flaws you want them to address. However, defer to their established process as much as possible—they'll already have a system they prefer, and it'll make both of your lives easier to follow it.

Finally, you'll also need to set some expectations around your timeline and what readers can expect from you. For instance, are you going to send beta readers your entire manuscript at once, or will you send it a few chapters at a time? How should they structure their feedback, and should they reference page numbers or chapters when taking notes? Perhaps it would be better for them to mark up your manuscript itself?

Additionally, what format will you share your draft in? Double spaced PDFs or Word documents are common, but it's always worth asking what will make your readers' lives as easy as possible—after all, no one wants to get an email two days before feedback is due, asking why a file won't open!

Speaking of feedback being due, you'll also want to set some deadlines, and every author structures these a bit differently. For example, because of my crazy publishing schedule, I'm known for sending manuscripts to my beta readers with only a week before I need their feedback returned to me. Fortunately, my beta readers are tremendously patient and overall awesome people—I'm very lucky in that regard.

However, this is one of those do as I say, not as I do kind of situations. If at all possible, try to leave about a month between when you send your manuscript to readers and when you ask for it back. Likewise, sit down and talk through your schedule with your critique partner to decide on a deadline that works for both of you. Remember, they'll expect you to critique their manuscript in return, so ensure you have enough time to do your best work. If you're working with specific beta reader or critique groups, ask what system they use and follow their normal procedure—it's just common courtesy.

Similarly, editors will have their own systems as well, and they'll be able to tell you more about their turnaround time and process during your initial consultation. Do your best to follow all the guidelines they give you, including things like paying on time, sending your manuscript in the correct format, and showing up to any meetings you schedule.

Last but not least, don't be afraid to send polite reminders to your readers as their deadline approaches. With beta readers especially, you can expect that at least a few of them will fail to send their feedback to you in a timely manner, or at all—however, some of them just need a gentle reminder. Always be respectful, but don't be afraid of becoming a squeaky wheel if you need to. Above all, make sure you're upholding your end of the bargain too! If you agreed to review someone else's novel or critique their manuscript, do so and send it back to them by the deadline you agreed on, if not earlier. You can't expect them to be reliable and trustworthy if you aren't willing to do the same.

The Goals of the Second Rest

Finally, with your readers locked down and your schedule set, it's time to rest.

This whole process of making connections and gathering feedback inevitably takes a month or two, so I encourage you to use this time to relax and recharge your creative brain. That means you shouldn't keep editing your novel—don't even skim through it. You need this time not only to rest, but to gain another solid dose of objectivity towards your story as well. Just like you needed to take a break between writing your first draft and starting your second, you also want to take a break before you have to process your readers' feedback. I promise it'll make the process easier in the long run, even if it seems like wasted time now.

Of course, if you're still itching to do something that will improve your writing, take this time to read. I'm sure you've set aside a few books while working on this challenge, so use this as the perfect opportunity to catch up on your backlog. After all, not only is reading good for your soul, but it's a great way to learn more about storytelling too!

So, pick up a good book, store your manuscript in a drawer for a few weeks, and come back once you've gathered the feedback you need. It won't be long before your novel is complete, so savor this last bit of rest while you can.

When you return we'll begin applying the feedback you've gathered from readers, but for now, here are your goals for the Second Rest:

1. Choose which readers work best for you: beta readers, critique partners, or professional editors.
2. Reach out to two or more of these groups about reviewing your manuscript.
3. Set the right expectations around what kind of feedback you need, any deadlines you have, and what you'll do in return.

4. Take some time to rest and recharge while you wait for feedback.

On to Day Seven!

10

DAY SEVEN: FACING THE OUTSIDE WORLD

Day Seven is a strange day in the scope of this challenge, because it carries a striking similarity to many of the other days you've already experienced—from Day One to Days Three and Four, the gang's all here.

You see, you've been away from your novel for at least a week or two, meaning you're returning with fresh eyes. Not only that, but you're also coming back to what will likely be pages of feedback to process and consider, much like you faced at the start of this challenge. Of course, as was the case in those early days, you won't necessarily like everything you find either.

While the beginning of this challenge should have helped you catch most of the flaws in your manuscript, there will inevitably be things you missed that your readers picked up on during the Second Rest. Sifting through that feedback is a major task, and one you want to approach with care. It's easy to get sucked in by every negative comment and hurt by each piece of criticism but, in reality, not all the feedback you received will be valuable—or even relevant to your story.

So, welcome back. Today you'll have to steel yourself as we face the final flaws in your novel, but don't worry. Just like we did throughout the start of this challenge, today we'll create an organized game plan to help you sort through these flaws and find the best ways to improve your story!

Learning to Handle Feedback

Before anything else can happen today, you'll want to start by making sure you've thanked your readers.

Whether they were a beta reader, your critique partner, or your editor, a gracious email or even a phone call is always appreciated. Make sure you've held up your end of the bargain too—if you agreed to critique their manuscript in exchange for their feedback, finish doing so before returning to your own story. Not only is this the respectful thing to do, but it prevents you from burning bridges you'll be happy to have in the future. It's always wise to stay in touch with any readers you enjoyed working with and to show your gratitude for all their help. You could even offer to send them a copy of your book once it's published—it's exciting to see a novel you helped work on come to fruition, and it's a nice physical reminder of how much you appreciate their time and effort.

Either way, say your thank yous before you start reading everyone's feedback—you might not be feeling so gracious afterwards!

While I'm mostly kidding, it is true that processing your readers' feedback won't be easy. Criticism is never fun—no matter how constructive—and because of this, it's important that you start this process from the right head space.

For starters, any criticism from your readers isn't personal, even if it feels that way right now. Ultimately, your story is a part of you, and it's easy to overreact to the flaws other people pointed out. The best thing you can do at this stage is to remind yourself to stay objective, and to look at this feedback through the eyes of an outsider.

Of course, this doesn't just apply to criticism either! Don't let compliments go to your head, because these positive notes can quickly become just as damaging as the negative ones. You need to remain objective, and puffing yourself up over the praise you received is a fast track to failing on that front.

My best suggestion for avoiding both of these knee-jerk reactions is to read all the feedback you received—whether from your editor, beta readers, or critique partner—en masse. Then step away for a few hours. If you review this feedback in the morning and return to handle it in the evening, you'll give your subconscious the time it needs to sort through your emotions and organize your thoughts. Not only is this good for your stress levels, but it'll make it that much easier to process this feedback with a level head.

From there, all that's left to do is tackle the intimidating process of actually sorting through all this feedback.

Depending on how many readers you worked with, you could have anywhere from a few suggestions to dozens of pages of notes to consider. Fortunately, just like you organized your own thoughts through your reverse outline earlier in this challenge, you'll be able to follow a similar process here.

Making Sense of It All

Facing a massive wall of feedback is undoubtedly stressful, so weeding out the slush pile will be our first order of business. By the end of this process, you'll have turned your feedback into a more usable plan, just like the one you created back on Day Four.

To begin this process, spread out all the feedback you've received and open up to a blank page in your reverse outline. Write the date and label the page appropriately.

Then start by going through your feedback and fixing all the minor issues you find: typos, spelling mistakes, missing punctuation, and the like. If you got a lot of comments about a specific error, make a note of that in your reverse outline to take care of later. These general fixes should be quick to complete, especially if your readers were diligent about supplying page numbers when leaving feedback. Though this round of editing isn't for correcting minor mistakes like these, you'll probably still end up with a few notes about them, and you might as well fix them while they're at the top of your mind. The worst-case scenario is that you waste five minutes correcting errors you'll end up cutting out anyways, but ideally you'll have saved yourself a bit of time when you sit down to proofread in a few days. Either way, quickly remove these small items from your list of feedback to make the whole thing a bit more manageable.

Next up, you'll want to organize your remaining feedback. Your readers will have likely commented on the same flaws multiple times, and this can quickly inflate the amount of information you have to sort through to an unreasonable level. Fortunately, the best remedy for this is simply to transfer this feedback to your reverse outline itself, giving you the opportunity to categorize and manage everything you've received.

Start by writing down these five categories, each on their own blank page in your reverse outline:

- **Plot:** Everything related to your story's structure, plot holes, or core conflict.
- **Character Development:** Notes about your characters' arcs, personalities, backgrounds, and behavior.
- **Worldbuilding:** Feedback on believability or inconsistencies in your story.
- **Pacing:** Anything related to chapter structure, scenes, or rushed/slow sections of your story.
- **Other:** A space for general notes about your story, including tense, point of view, theme, tone, and overall quality.

Then transfer each piece of feedback to the most applicable category, retaining any page numbers your readers may have mentioned—this will make your life much easier later on. Plus, don't forget to include compliments and praise as well!

Alongside transferring these notes, you'll also want to quickly jot down who gave you that piece of feedback—your editor, a beta reader, or a critique partner? This will allow you to better understand the perspective each comment is coming from, and will make it easier to deal with repeat feedback. Now, when a piece of feedback comes up multiple times, you won't need to rewrite it—instead, simply make a note of who mentioned it along with any extra details they may have provided.

By the time you've organized all of this feedback in your reverse outline, you'll have done a few things. First, you'll have likely shrunk your list of feedback by a significant amount, just by combining duplicate material. You'll also have everything organized into common sections, making them far easier to review. Last but not least, you'll have forced yourself to think more clearly about each comment you received, without the pressure of immediately putting that feedback into action.

Hopefully, this process has helped you get a good idea of what flaws stand out the most in your story, meaning you can now start actually dealing with some of this feedback.

For starters, go through your list and cross out any feedback that is unusable or inaccurate. Then, put an asterisk or other mark beside anything you're unsure of, and highlight the ones you definitely plan to fix. Of course, you need to be brutally honest with yourself here, especially when crossing items off your list. There's a difference between genuinely wrong feedback, and just something you disagree with. While you don't need to put every piece of advice you received into action, it is worth considering why your reader mentioned it to begin with—especially if it's a comment you've gotten from multiple people. If this feedback showed up two or even three times from different readers, give it a bit of extra thought before writing it off.

In a similar vein, you may feel like some of your readers are trying to "change your story," or that they don't understand your ideas, voice, or style. This is completely understandable and also entirely possible—readers are only human, and each will approach your story from their own unique perspective. Again, this is one more place where you'll need to be objective. Some of the feedback you received won't be valuable and can be crossed out right away, but some of it might genuinely reflect things you can improve in your story —even if it's something you disagree with at first glance.

Fortunately, there is one question you can ask to help you decide what feedback to focus on and what you can safely ignore—who did it come from?

You see, as I mentioned during the Second Rest, the various groups of readers you worked with will each have their own strengths and weaknesses. Beta readers are great resources en masse, but their individual comments might not always be the most valuable in isolation. Likewise, critique partners tend to be more reliable, but this can really depend on who you're working with and their personal level of writing skill. An editor, on the other hand, is someone you should almost always listen to. They're coming at your story from a place of expertise and experience, and if they say your story has a major flaw, that's worth paying attention to. Ideally, they'll have explained their reasoning whenever possible, but if not, it never hurts to shoot them a quick email if you're uncertain about a comment they left.

Of course, all of these groups can make mistakes, or might simply have the wrong idea about your story. At the end of the day, you as the author make the final decision.

Still, when reviewing the feedback you received, consider adding a bit of extra weight to anything multiple readers or an editor took note of. For feedback from beta readers specifically, pay attention to the trends in their feedback, as this can clue you into broader problems that your target audience will also pick up on down the road.

All of this holds true when reviewing the feedback you marked with an asterisk as well. Think carefully about whether this advice could really benefit your story and what affect it would have on your core idea. Is it a minor change, or a plot breaking one? Does it come from multiple people and does it relate closely to a piece of feedback you already planned to put into action? Again, this is one of those places where you'll need to do some soul searching and make some tough decisions about your story.

Either way, by the end of this process your entire list of feedback should be organized into two camps—the ones you crossed out, and the ones you highlighted.

Another Optional Rest

With your list of feedback organized and sorted through, you can start applying these changes to your story. If everything went well during the beginning of this challenge, you hopefully won't have a ton of major changes to make here—but it's also possible you will.

If you ended this process with pages and pages of changes to work through, this will naturally take some time, and you want to give each item on your list the proper amount of attention. After all, the goal of this is to improve your novel, and only time and patient revision can fix major problems. So, just like the optional rest we had back on Day Five, today you'll get another chance to temporarily pause this challenge and put some of this feedback into action—*if* you need to.

Ultimately, regardless of whether you plan to take advantage of this optional rest or not, you'll want to approach your list of feedback in a similar way. Start by handling the things you know are an easy fix, just to get them off your plate. Then take some time to research and consider anything you aren't sure how to fix. You may find that flipping back to the list of questions we reviewed on Day Four can help with this, so feel free to read through those as you shape your thoughts.

From there, it's simply a matter of tackling each piece of feedback one by one. Just like we've done throughout the rest of this challenge, I always recommend focusing on the big-picture problems first, and then slowly narrowing your focus to specific chapters and scenes as you progress. You'll also want to make sure you keep your reverse outline up to date whenever you make changes, both to stay organized and to make sure you aren't breaking another part of your story in the process.

As difficult as some of this feedback may be to address, continue marching forward until you've checked everything off your list and your draft is in a place you're happy with. If you need to take advantage of this optional rest, I'll see you again in a few days—if not, then you're ready to call your story done!

The Goals of Day Seven

With Day Seven at its end, you've officially finished your third draft and—in terms of your story itself—your novel has reached its final form.

Before you wrap up for today, I hope you'll take a moment to look back over your story and your writing journey so far. Think back to where you were when you had only just finished your first draft and compare that to now. Though I can't say anything for certain, I imagine your story is far stronger than you ever thought it could be, thanks to all the hard work and time you've put into it.

While we need a few final layers of polish to complete your fourth and final draft, it won't be much longer before your novel is ready to hand to the world!

Tomorrow we'll start editing your novel's prose, but for now, here are the goals you've completed for Day Seven:

1. Read through the feedback you received during the Second Rest and then step away for a while to clear your head.
2. Transfer this feedback to your reverse outline, organizing it by category.
3. Cross out any feedback you plan to ignore and highlight the ones you know you'll use.
4. Apply this highlighted feedback to your story.

On to Day Eight!

11

DAY EIGHT: A FINAL COAT OF PAINT

When it comes to developing your writing skills, a lot of people have the wrong impression. On the one hand, many believe good storytelling is something that can only be achieved through a magical stroke of genius, not something you can study and learn from books and teachers. At the same time though, those writers also think the secret to perfect prose is mastering English grammar and memorizing their thesaurus. In reality, they've got both equations backwards.

Storytelling is an art form—prose is a muscle memory.

Almost all aspects of good storytelling can be taught, just like painting or sculpture, while mastering your prose is something you have to learn through practice, patience, and more practice. Sure, you need a basic understanding of English grammar and spelling, but beyond that most of the choices you'll face in terms of your prose are stylistic.

This can frustrate for a lot of writers, because they've spent months and years studying the *correct* way to write, only to realize they're no closer to discovering their *own* writing voice. There really is nothing quite like practice and experience when it comes to developing these skills.

Of course, we're at the point in this challenge when your prose can finally become your priority, and there will undoubtedly be room for you to tweak and improve what you've written so far. Day Eight is your chance to put those improvements into action, though you won't find many grammar or spelling tricks here—instead, today will be all about helping you strengthen the voice of your story.

The Many Forms of Editing

With your third draft complete, you can finally set your story aside—meaning now is the time to focus on your prose.

In all likelihood, you'll have quite a few problems with your prose thanks to lingering remnants from earlier drafts and the constant shuffle caused by the many rounds of rewrites you've gone through. Fortunately, most of these problems will fall into a few common categories, making it much easier to root them out.

While this might look similar to the editing you did earlier in the challenge at first glance, this process will go a bit differently. Now that your third draft is complete, our focus is no longer on your story itself, but on how you tell that story. This means we'll be dealing with everything from writing style to clarity, and tomorrow we'll wrap up by focusing on the final stage of editing—proofreading.

Of course, as you go through today's goals you'll probably come across some spelling errors, typos, and grammatical mistakes, and it's well worth your time to fix those when you find them. This will save you time tomorrow, and it'll make it that much less likely that you'll miss these errors in the long run. Still, today's focus is less on those technical writing skills, and more on the flow, rhythm, and readability of your manuscript as a whole.

However, even that's not the limit to what we'll be dealing with today.

While yes, you want your writing to be coherent and clear, there's more to editing your prose than just cleaning up your writing style. You'll also want to refine your voice as an author by questioning what defines your authorial voice in the first place.

As intimidating and ethereal as that sounds—because again, prose is something you learn through practice—approaching this one chapter at a time will make everything go much more smoothly. That's where today's goals will really differ from previous ones. Instead of going through your manuscript all at once, we'll be working chapter by chapter based on four categories:

- Descriptions
- Dialog
- Voice
- Excess

Like I keep saying, writing compelling prose is about so much more than a set of rules, and it's something you develop your own style and flair for over time. Still, I'm going to do my best to provide some basic guidelines to help get you started, letting you build your own writing voice from there.

So, open your manuscript and flip to the first chapter. We'll begin there.

Capturing the Details

A big part of what shapes your story is how you describe it. These descriptions will encompass everything from your settings and characters, to events, objects, creatures, cultures, and more. The way you convey these details—the who, what, when, where, why, and how—will define how your reader experiences your story. This means that your descriptions need to serve your story above all else, without a lot of fluff to clutter the landscape.

Of course, you've probably written and rewritten the descriptions in your story at least a few times by now, so you'll likely have some excess left over from earlier drafts. To account for that, we're going to hone in on the most compelling details within your manuscript and highlight those for your reader—specifically focusing on the two types of descriptions that will dominate your story:

———

Settings:

When describing locations in your story, your main goal is to capture the feeling of that place above and beyond just sights and sounds. Not only that, but you also want to introduce any important objects or features that will influence your plot later on.

To do this, consider all five human senses, and pick one or two that best capture the tone and key details of each setting.

For example, sights and sounds make sense to describe a dimly lit room, letting you paint a picture of a dark, quiet, and perhaps eerie space. On the other hand, a sewer almost demands to be described using smell, but touch would work too. The slimy walls and slick tile floor can really give your reader a strong sense of how gross this space is, while simultaneously setting up the slippery fall your protagonist is about to suffer from!

Of course, certain characters will prefer certain senses, and this can be a great way to add some individual flair to your cast. For instance, a vampire will probably describe locations using their sense of smell because that sense is stronger, while a character who is blind definitely won't describe locations based on sight. Again, this is one more way to infuse your story with important information, without requiring excessive exposition.

Characters:

Just like with settings, the way you describe your characters is about more than physical appearance—it's about how they act and feel to be around, along with the impressions they leave on others.

Unfortunately, writers can often lean so heavily on physical traits that their characters become nothing but a hodgepodge of blonde, pale, short, bouncy, and blue-eyed. However, what does that really tell us about that character? Other than their looks, not much, giving us a very shallow impression of who they are.

Because of this, when describing your characters—especially when you first introduce them—you want to focus on more than what they look like. Think about their core personality traits and how they communicate those traits through their body language, movements, and behavior.

As an example, an aggressive or domineering character might be shown pushing others to the side, talking over other people, or needing to be in the middle of every group.

None of these descriptions have anything to do with what they look like, yet you can still visualize them in your mind thanks to that sense of movement. Plus, a shy or more gracious character wouldn't act that way, making their personality that much more distinct. Throw in one or two standout physical traits and your reader will walk away with a powerful understanding of that character, regardless of what they look like.

———

Of course, sometimes it's hard to visualize either your settings or your characters, which makes it even harder to describe them to your reader. This is where brainstorming comes into play, since you'll need to develop a strong sense of these elements before you can adequately describe them.

Flipping through your first chapter, look for locations or cast members you don't have a strong mental image of. If there are any, take some time to search around the internet for photos, drawings, music, or words that you think might fit— if you're following along from *The Ten Day Outline,* you can use your existing collection for this task. Specifically, try to focus on things that evoke the feeling or tone of what you're trying to describe, rather than looking for specific landmarks or physical traits. This will give you a stronger sense of what it feels like to experience that person or place, which is ultimately the goal when writing descriptions.

Really, what this all boils down to is the age old advice of "show, don't tell,"

At its core, this simple phrase is a great reminder to let your readers truly experience the events, characters, and settings of your story. Rather than telling them "the wide open field was beautiful," it's far more compelling to show them how the wind brushed through the tall grasses and the blue sky spread out across the valley. They'll not only understand the beauty of this location firsthand, but they'll also know what it feels like to be there.

Think of your job as being similar to that of a 4D movie camera. Movies can't tell us the main character is sad, so instead they show us through body language, dialog, and behavior. A location isn't simply described as luxurious— rather, we're shown the glittering neon lights and the buzzing lines of glamorous cars. The same principles apply to your own novel. As you're reviewing your first chapter, think carefully about how you're describing each location and character you introduce. Are you showing, or telling?

Thankfully, shifting from one to the other isn't too difficult —it's really just a matter of hunting down overused adjectives and adverbs. Personally, I recommend going through your first chapter and highlighting every place you catch yourself telling rather than showing. Then, fix these places by focusing more on movement and behavior, as well as the five senses. As you go, you'll get a better idea of how to address these problems quickly, picking up speed by the end of the chapter.

Of course, not all telling is bad, and this is where getting a feel for your own writing voice comes into play. There's a balance to be struck here and sometimes telling is the right choice when you just need to get a point across. You want to keep your story moving without a ton of excess prose to slow your reader down, and showing naturally takes up more space on the page.

Really, there are no hard and fast rules when it comes to showing versus telling—instead, you'll need to listen to your story and think about the purpose of each description you come across. Are you painting a picture for your reader, or just conveying some quick facts before moving on?

Last but not least, there's one more category of descriptions you'll want to pay attention to in your manuscript—your characters' emotions.

As a general rule, major emotional moments are one place where telling is never justified, because these emotional shifts are some of the most fragile and impactful passages in your entire novel. Think of the hotspots you created back on Day Three when your plot and character arcs overlapped— these are where you'll find your story's strongest emotional shifts, because your characters are undergoing major trials and moments of growth. These will naturally shake them, and will force them to wrestle with their own feelings.

For instance, consider a scene where a character grieves another character's death or rethinks their own worldview after witnessing something heartwrenching. These moments need to be shown to give them the weight they deserve, making this an important time to lean on symbolism, body language, and reflection.

Fortunately, there shouldn't be many of these emotional shifts in your first chapter, so you won't need to worry about them just yet. Instead, take this first chapter as a chance to get used to the differences between showing and telling, and look for these major moments closer to your story's plot points as we move forward.

Polishing Your Dialog

With your story's descriptions in a solid place, you can turn to your dialog.

Dialog is one of those things that many, *many* writers struggle with, because it can be incredibly difficult to capture the way people speak through the written word. To compound this difficulty, you don't actually want your written dialog to perfectly match spoken language—after all, you'd end up with a whole lot of ums, uhs, and awkward pauses if you did!

Instead, your goal when writing dialog is to create a hybrid of sorts, combining the feel of spoken words with the clarity and ease of reading that comes from written language.

A big part of this is ensuring your characters each have their own unique voices. For some characters, that'll have a lot to do with regional dialects and accents, but many writers can go overboard here. Most of the time, leaning heavily on misspellings and regional pronunciations is ill advised, and works best when used sparingly. I strongly encourage you to review any dialog you've written with a distinct accent, both to ensure your character's meaning is clear and to make sure you're not creating a caricature out of an otherwise fully fledged character.

Rather than relying on dialog tricks, a better option is to give individual voices to each of your characters by focusing on their personalities. A character who is shy or anxious won't talk the same way as one who is aggressive and domineering —it's simply not in their personality.

The other goal here is consistency. You want characters to speak with their own voice from beginning to end, but it's easy to accidentally let them slip into another character's voice—or your own voice—as your story goes on. For most characters, reading their dialog aloud will be enough to give you a good feel for how it flows and whether it still captures that character's personality.

However, if you run into a character whose dialog you just can't nail down, you'll need to take more drastic measures. To do this, skim through your entire manuscript and highlight every line of dialog that character speaks. Then read them back to back and listen to how it sounds. Often, by reading their entire story's worth of dialog at once, you'll quickly find where you went astray and be able to remedy the problem.

Of course, alongside giving your characters their own voices, you also need to consider your dialog tags.

Dialog tags are often a contentious subject, with some people mixing in everything from whispered to yelled, screamed, shouted, murmured, and even soliloquized. On the other hand, many writers insist that "said" is the only tag that should ever—and I mean *ever*—follow a line of dialog.

In reality, the truth is somewhere in the middle. The majority of the time, said is more than enough to convey your meaning, and the tone of your dialog should primarily be gleaned from the dialog itself rather than the dialog tag. However, sometimes more descriptive dialog tags can be valuable, so long as they're used in moderation—again, it really depends on your writing style.

Either way, it's well worth your time to review your dialog tags to see if you're overusing them. Ideally, dialog tags should melt into the background of your story, serving more to frame what's being said rather than to dominate it. In fact, even "said" can become overbearing. Leaving your dialog without a tag—so long as it's still clear who is speaking—can be done to great effect, especially during long conversations when your readers would otherwise be seeing "said" dozens of times in a row.

Alternatively, if you find yourself craving more flair than "said" can provide, consider attaching some descriptions to your dialog. For instance, instead of "he whispered," a better option could be "he said, his voice barely registering in the room." Ultimately, whether this works will depend on the importance of that description in setting the scene for your reader, just like it did for the other descriptions we covered.

Discovering Your Own Voice

At this point, we've talked a lot about your writing voice in relation to other aspects of your story, but it's also something worth considering in isolation.

To a large extent, your writing voice is something you'll develop naturally over time. The more you write, the more you'll cultivate the muscle memory that shapes how you structure your prose. However, sometimes different stories will require a slightly different voice, and this largely comes down to the tone and mood of your story. For instance, a classic horror writer will have a distinctly somber, dark, and suspenseful writing voice—a voice that wouldn't mesh well with a lighthearted coming of age adventure. Likewise, a cozy romance would feel more lighthearted, emotional, wistful, or even exciting thanks to its voice.

Depending on what type of story you're creating, take a moment to consider your word choice and style. Does it share a common identity with your story's subject matter? Does the tone of each scene make sense for its intended intensity and its place within your story? Above all, does your writing voice make sense within your novel's genre?

Really, you can boil this down to the difference between two words: cut and eviscerate.

Both terms mean essentially the same thing, yet they create entirely different mental images and are appropriate for entirely different stories. These kinds of small decisions will shape your writing voice, so you want to choose your words carefully. Fortunately, the best way to catch these nuances is fairly simple—just read your manuscript aloud, or even set your computer up to read it for you. Not only will this help you focus, but you'll also be able to hear when something sounds off.

If the tone of your writing matches your story's subject and the voice you want to create, you're good to go. If not, pull out the thesaurus and take some time to refine your word choice until it better matches your vision for your story.

Learning to Trust Your Readers

Last but not least, it's time to trim the fat from your prose.

As you've gone through each of the sections above, you've hopefully found that most of the weaknesses in your writing were fairly straightforward to fix—with some rewording and basic clean up, your descriptions, dialog, and even authorial voice can see huge improvements. However, some sections of your prose might not be so easily dealt with, and this is no truer than when it comes to excess.

You see, some sections of your prose will simply be extra, either repeating information you've already covered or focusing on details that don't truly matter. Yet, you may struggle to cut these passages from your manuscript. You put in the hard work to write them, so why scrap them now?

Well, even in the best-case scenario, these sections of your manuscript don't add anything of value. Descriptions that fail to capture the feeling of a place or physical attributes that say nothing about a character should all be cut from your story, or at least substantially rewritten. Likewise, you probably need to rethink excessive dialog tags that clutter or overwhelm your characters' voices. You even want to avoid excess when conveying information to your readers, rather than repeating the same descriptions, exposition, and explanations ad nauseam.

What this comes down to is learning to trust your readers.

Repeating walls of information over and over may not add value to your story, but it does signal that you don't trust your readers to keep up with what's happening on the page. At best, this slows the pacing of your story to a crawl, and at worst it feels patronizing and insulting. Much like showing your reader a setting rather than telling them about it, there's simply a better way to handle this.

Of course, you probably won't run into this problem much while reviewing your first chapter, since everything is new and relevant at that stage in your story. However, as you get deeper into your manuscript, it may come up more often. While you always want your story to be clear and cohesive, there's rarely a need to retread old information that your reader already understands—especially more than twice.

So, if you find yourself repeating the same exposition without adding anything new, ask yourself why.

Is it because something has changed that you need to alert readers to, or is it just because you don't trust them to keep up? If it's the latter, pause for a moment and recognize that your readers are smarter than you think—give them the information they need to connect the dots on their own, and then trust that they'll understand.

The Goals of Day Eight

Once you've finished reviewing your first chapter, you can move on to your second, third, fourth, and so on, until you've tackled all four categories for every chapter in your novel.

At first, this may seem impossible to complete quickly, but you should find yourself getting faster and faster as you tackle each successive chapter. After all, the problems you run into early on will likely come up again later in your manuscript, until you instinctively know what to look for as you flip to a new chapter.

Ultimately, by the time this process is complete you'll not only have a more polished novel, but a stronger sense of your own writing voice.

Still, this is a hard thing to pin down and almost an impossible thing to teach. Unlike storytelling, prose is really something you develop a feel for over time. If you find that your prose isn't perfect, even after all of this work, that's ok.

As with so many art forms, each successive project you work on will be better than the last, until eventually you become a master. However, to reach that level requires you to keep writing and keep creating. In that way, Day Eight serves two dual purposes—it helps you polish and strengthen your writing, but it also prevents you from obsessing over your prose forever. Focus instead on what you know how to improve and just keep moving forward—the rest will come together in time.

Tomorrow we'll put the finishing touches on your novel, but for now, here are the goals you've completed for Day Eight:

1. Starting with your first chapter, consider how you describe the locations, events, and characters within your story.
2. Polish your draft's dialog and dialog tags, trying to capture your characters' unique voices.
3. Refine your word choice to reflect the tone of your story and trim away any excess exposition.
4. Once you've finished your first chapter, complete this process for every other chapter in your manuscript.

On to Day Nine!

12

DAY NINE: CREATING A WORTHY COMPETITOR

W hether you plan to publish traditionally or self-publish, you may have heard rumblings about how "unprofessional" or "amateur" self-published novels are. This is less common these days, but in the early era of e-readers many people harbored a lot of negative feelings towards independent authors and their work.

Why, you might ask?

Well, self-published authors often didn't have access to a lot of the editorial support structures that were available at traditional publishing houses. It wasn't that their stories were of a lesser quality, or that they weren't talented writers, or even that their novels weren't worth reading—most of the time, it just meant their books hadn't been proofread. This left their otherwise good stories cluttered with typos, misspellings, and other errors, giving their novels a less than professional feel.

These days, however, that simply doesn't have to be the case. Authors have more access to editors and tools than ever before, and most readers can no longer tell the difference between self-published and traditionally published novels. Both have the level of quality we expect from professionals, because both types of authors *are* professionals.

Ultimately, regardless of how you plan to publish your novel, readers and agents alike expect your work to be proofread out of the gate. Without this final level of polish, you're selling your story short and making it that much harder for your novel to succeed. It's no longer about competition between self-published and traditionally published novels— instead, you're competing with both.

Fortunately, proofreading doesn't have to be hard. By putting in the time and knowing what to look for, you can polish these final details of your manuscript and end up creating a novel that can stand toe to toe with any other book out there!

Your Personal Style Guide

When it comes to proofreading your novel, it's all in the details. A lot of this comes down to spell checking your manuscript and fixing common problems like passive voice or incorrect grammar, but it also has a lot to do with consistency—names should be spelled the same and objects, languages, and details need to be cohesive.

Unfortunately, when you're dealing with a fifty thousand word manuscript, that's no small feat. Heck, even keeping track of whether you spelled hotspots as "hot spots" or "hotspots" in a forty thousand word non-fiction book about editing is hard enough—ask me how I know!

This is where creating a style guide for your novel becomes really valuable. In fact, style guides are commonly used in the traditional publishing world for this exact purpose, and it's well worth your time to create one for your own story. This will help you manage everything from names and spellings, to formatting, tense, and punctuation, ensuring all of it is consistent and cohesive within your manuscript.

Best of all, you've completed a lot of this work already. For the most part, your story rulebook from all the way back on Day Two will contain a lot of the information you need for your style guide, making this process that much easier.

To start your style guide, list this information with their official spellings, usages, and capitalizations:

- Place names
- Character names
- Spell, item, technology, and other object names
- Names of historical events
- Pronouns for each character
- Any constructed languages you've created

In addition to these things, you'll also want to record your story's tense. This is one of the harder parts of proofreading, because tense switching is very easy to overlook. Essentially, it's when you flip between difference tenses within the same story, without a good reason for doing so. By this point, you should have committed to a single tense, but if you're unsure what tense that is here's a quick breakdown:

- **Past Tense:** I ran, they walked, it saw, et cetera…
  This is one of the most common tenses used in fiction, and it's a good option for almost any story. It's versatile and unobtrusive, and most readers are used to seeing stories told in this tense.
- **Present Tense:** I run, they walk, it sees, et cetera…

This is another common tense used in novels, especially when the author wants readers to feel the immediacy of a story's action. Present Tense allows everything to unfold in the moment, though that does mean characters can't reflect on things that haven't yet happened in your story, which is possible with Past Tense.

- **Future Tense:** I will run, they will walk, it will see, et cetera… Writers rarely use this tense in fiction, and it's really best for experimental or literary novels. Think carefully about whether or not Future Tense fits your story before choosing this option.

Out of these three, you're likely already using either past or present tense, and there is rarely a compelling reason to change your novel's tense at this stage. Both are flexible enough to work with almost any story, so your focus at this point should on be making sure you're staying consistent—just like with everything else in your style guide. Unless you feel strongly that a different tense would better suit your story, simply record the tense you're currently using in your style guide.

By the time you're done with this, your style guide might not be particularly long, and that's ok. Even half a page is fine, so long as you cover all the information necessary. Of course, for novels with a lot of worldbuilding, this could quickly grow into a much larger document. That's ok too—if you have more unique names and words to keep track of, they'll naturally take up more space.

Either way, once your style guide is complete you can begin using it to proofread your novel, keeping it on hand as a reminder of how to spell and use these words and terms. Better yet, use the "find" and "replace" features in your word processor to hunt down these terms en masse, ensuring they're all capitalized and used correctly in much less time. When it comes to handling your novel's tense, that will require a bit more explanation.

Moving Past the Basics

Checking that the names and unique terms in your novel are spelled correctly is a pretty straightforward process and, like I mentioned, you can usually do this with the "find" function in most modern word processors. However, proofreading goes far beyond just spelling, and this is where today's goals get more complex.

Not only will you need to ensure you've spelled names correctly, but you'll also need to check your manuscript for incorrect grammar, missing punctuation, typos, tense switching, passive voice, and more. Fortunately, these are all things a spell checker or proofreading software can help you with, but even with those tools by your side this is still a slow and tedious process. Imagine having to read your entire manuscript, remaining laser focused on every letter, word, and comma—that's what proofreading is all about, and it's understandably exhausting.

Ideally, you won't have that many lingering errors in your draft, especially since you've already edited it so extensively throughout this challenge. Still, you're almost guaranteed to have at least a few flaws remaining, and these problems warrant your attention. If you want to create a novel that can stand up to any professionally published book, you'll need to root these out. Beyond the basics of spelling, grammar, and punctuation, here are some other things to look for when proofreading your novel:

———

Tense Switching:

As I hinted at previously, tense switching is when you switch between past and present tense without reason.

Often, this tense switching is purely accidental, and you may not even notice yourself doing it when you're writing. However, it's also very confusing for your reader and is overall bad form. As you proofread your manuscript, check to make sure your tense is consistent. If you ever do change tense midway through your story, ask yourself why. Does the story justify this change in tense, or was it an accident?

Passive Voice:

In case you're unfamiliar with the concept of passive or active voice, let's start with some quick definitions:

- **Passive Voice:** This is when a sentence's verb acts on the subject, resulting in more roundabout phrasing. For example, "My car was cleaned today."
- **Active Voice:** This is when a sentence's subject performs the verb, making the sentence feel more direct and clear. For example, "I cleaned my car today."

While the writing community often rails on passive voice, there's nothing actually *wrong* with using passive voice—you just want to do so in moderation. If you can rewrite your sentences in active voice and they still sound natural to your reader, you'll not only be making your writing more direct, but stronger as well. On the other hand, if you can't find a way to rewrite a passive sentence while keeping the same flow and meaning, that's ok too.

Ultimately, this is another place where you'll have to use your best judgment, while remembering that—as a general rule—active voice is the way to go.

Italics:

Italics are common in fiction, but they're often used in different ways. Sometimes italics can denote internal thoughts or an inner monologue, and other times they're used to show emphasis. Figure out how you're using them in your story—if you are—and keep them consistent.

Dialog:

When proofreading dialog, there are a few formatting concerns to pay attention to. Let's look at an example so you can see what I mean:

"It's ok," she said, doing her best to calm the fuming toddler. "You can tell me."

In response, they stomped their foot, crossing their arms tighter across their chest. "No!"

"All right, if you insist."

She walked away. She had been a parent long enough to know that, by simply ignoring them, they'd get bored of throwing their tantrum soon enough. She would figure out what was bothering them later, when they were in the mood to talk.

Notice how each line is separated. Whenever you shift to a new speaker, you want to skip down a line—this signals to your reader that a new person is talking, and makes the dialog easier to keep up with. When the person speaking has a specific dialog tag or action that accompanies their dialog, you should include that in the same line as well. However, when you shift back to normal action, you'll want to skip a line again, which you can see in the last paragraph of this example.

Additionally, pay attention to your punctuation. When finishing a line of dialog, the punctuation goes inside the quotation marks. When that dialog is followed by a dialog tag, you'll usually end it with a comma, unless it ends with either a question mark or an exclamation point. Finally, when dialog is split by a tag, the tag will end in a period rather than the usual comma—as you can see in the first sentence of our example.

Run-on Sentences:

To some extent, this is a stylistic concern—some writers favor short, sharp writing, while others like to indulge in long, flowing sentences. Genre can also come into play here, with some genres heavily favoring one style over the other.

Either way, regardless of which end of this spectrum you fall on, you should always aim to make your writing as clear as possible. As a general rule of thumb, avoid run-on sentences whenever you can, and always keep your reader's experience in mind.

Sentence Variety:

Speaking of sentence length, you don't want too many short sentences all in a row either. Think of it this way—every sentence you write ends with a stop sign in the form of a period. If you have too many stop signs clustered together, your reader will have to slam on the breaks so often they'll get whiplash.

Instead, strike a balance by varying your sentence length, creating a more engaging and rhythmic reading experience. Fortunately, reading your manuscript aloud is a great way to catch sections that lack this variety. Listen to the flow of your writing and try to include a variety of both short and long sentences where appropriate.

Scene Breaks:

Scene breaks are the decorative marks that separate the various scenes within your chapters, though there are a variety of ways they could apply to your novel. Most of the time, they're used to show when the story is transitioning to a new scene, but they can also denote a transition in other ways, such as when your cast moves to a new location or when a significant period of time has passed. In this book, you'll find them before and after any large sections of information—like this one!

Of course, you may not use scene breaks at all. Some authors prefer to just leave two lines blank between their scenes, while others don't space their scenes out at all. Either way, this is all about improving your reader's experience, and keeping your scene breaks consistent is key.

————

Personally, I'm a developmental editor first and foremost, so proofreading has never been my expertise. Even still, I regularly proofread my writing with good results, before having a few of my beta readers review my manuscripts to catch any last mistakes. Enlisting a second set of eyes to help you is especially valuable during this process.

Because of that, this is another time when it can be very worthwhile to enlist the help of a professional—specifically, a professional proofreader. Hand off your style guide and manuscript and let them go through all of this hard work for you. Not only will their expertise and experience make this process go much more smoothly, but they'll also save your eyes from having to pick out every stray comma, rogue apostrophe, and sarcastic semicolon.

Unfortunately, as with hiring any professional, this will come with an investment of both time and money. You may not be able to justify that, in which case, proofreading is absolutely something you can do on your own. Not only do you have the bulk of today to go through this process, but you'll have a final bit of time tomorrow to catch any lingering mistakes. Grab a friend to skim through your manuscript when you're done, and you should be good to go.

If you plan to go it alone, then buckle down and open up your manuscript. With your style guide beside you, load your manuscript into the grammar checker of choice, or pull out a red pen and a hard copy of your novel. Reading through your story, you'll want to look for these things:

- Missing or incorrect punctuation
- Misspellings and misused words
- Grammatical mistakes
- Tense skipping
- Passive voice
- Formatting issues
- Sentence structure
- Rhythm
- Scene breaks
- Other Typos

Above all, don't be afraid to take your time going through this process. Work chapter by chapter, taking breaks when you need them and keeping in mind any repeat problems you find. If you run into an error in one place, you'll likely find it elsewhere too.

By the time you've reached your final chapter, you'll likely be exhausted, but stick with me for just a little longer. We aren't done for the day quite yet, but we're almost there.

The Perfect Opening Line

Out of all of your goals for today, proofreading is by far the hardest in terms of the time and energy required. Even still, finalizing your novel's opening line often *feels* the hardest in terms of sheer creative brain power.

While it's possible you already have an opening line you feel confident in, this is one sticking point almost all writers obsess over. Opening lines carry a lot of weight, both because of popular perception and because they act as your reader's first window into your story. Getting your opening line right is definitely important, but also it's not worth obsessing over.

Of course, you may wonder—if this is so important, why have we left it until the very end of the challenge?

Well, this was for a few reasons. For starters, you needed a complete understanding of your story to truly capture it in your opening line, and that didn't happen until just recently. Likewise, I didn't want you obsessing over this while your story was still in flux earlier on. And, finally, with your manuscript now proofread you should be more familiar with the errors you're prone to while writing. You can avoid all of those here, writing a strong and compelling opening line that truly represents your novel.

First and foremost, your opening line's job is to lead your reader into your story's world by capturing a specific image or sensation. This sets the tone for the rest of your novel and lays the groundwork you'll build on throughout the rest of your story. For example, here's the opening line from J. R. R. Tolkien's *The Hobbit*:

"In a hole in the ground there lived a hobbit. Not a nasty, dirty, wet hole, filled with the ends of worms and an oozy smell, nor yet a dry, bare, sandy hole with nothing in it to sit down on or to eat: it was a hobbit-hole, and that means comfort."

While this is technically an opening paragraph rather than an opening line, it serves essentially the same purpose. This opening perfectly encapsulates the whimsical, fantastical tone of this book, while also giving us our first image of this story's world—comfortable chairs, fireplaces, warm rooms, and soft rugs.

In contrast, the opening paragraph of Tolkien's *The Lord of the Rings: Return of the King* gives us a much darker, gloomier impression:

"Pippin looked out from the shelter of Gandalf's cloak. He wondered if he was awake or still sleeping, still in the swift-moving dream in which he had been wrapped so long since the great ride began. The dark world was rushing by and the wind sang loudly in his ears. He could see nothing but the wheeling stars, and away to his right vast shadows against the sky where the mountains of the South marched past. Sleepily he tried to reckon the times and stages of their journey, but his memory was drowsy and uncertain."

This opening paragraph feels dark and stormy, with frightening shadows lingering around the edges. The description of Pippin's memory as "drowsy and uncertain" lends everything a certain sense of anxiety as well—what a perfect way to prepare the reader for all the trials to come in this final book of Tolkien's trilogy!

When finalizing your own novel's opening, you'll want to capture this same strong image. To do this, start by listing four or five words that describe your story's tone and mood, along with the first image you want your readers to see. This could be a setting, object, event, or even a person—whatever you think best represents the story you're about to tell.

If you're struggling with this, try thinking of something unique or intriguing that your reader can develop an emotional connection to, even if it isn't a specific image. In *The Hobbit*, the phrase "and that means comfort" gives us an emotional link to our own perception of comfort, letting us fill in the gaps with feelings of warm fireplaces and safety. This comforting sensation deeply ties into the childlike wonder of this book, even though Tolkien leaves a lot of the details up to us as the reader.

Of course, as you work on your opening line, you may feel pressured to turn it into some kind of epic literary masterpiece, to which I say—don't.

There's really no need to get fancy with your novel's opening because, in reality, very few authors can pull off the kind of highbrow literary style seen in the classics—it simply won't match the more grounded genre fiction most of us write. This means there's no need to make sweeping statements about the nature of humanity or the purpose of life, unless this truly captures the essence of your story. Instead, focus on giving your reader an image and a feeling they can latch on to, one that encapsulates the adventure you're preparing to take them on. Better yet, make sure you can sum this up in a few impactful sentences. These are your promise to your reader, telling them, "here is what I'm about to give you."

Finally, if all else fails, try to surprise your reader. Say something that will confuse or intrigue them, so long as it remains relevant to your core story, such as Gabriel Garcia Marquez's famous opening to *One Hundred Years of Solitude*:

> "Many years later, as he faced the firing squad, Colonel Aureliano Buendía was to remember that distant afternoon when his father took him to discover ice."

With so many strong mental images to latch on to in this opening line—from firing squads to discovering ice—it's easy to see why this story sucks you in from the very start!

Bringing It All Together

Finally, with your opening line set in stone, your novel is complete—except not quite. There's still one last thing you'll need to do before your novel is truly finished, and that is choosing your novel's title.

While you may have decided on a title already, you might also be stuck with a working title you aren't quite happy with, so let's go over some quick tips for titling your novel.

First up, your novel's title is more of a sales tool than anything else. What you call your book will not only intrigue and interest your target readers, but will also signal to them what genre your novel is in. Likewise, your title makes a promise to your reader about what they're about to experience—just like your opening line, your Hook, and your first chapter. Because of this, it's important to ensure your novel's title is consistent with your genre and the story you're telling. This will not only make it easier for your target readers to find you, but it'll also ensure you're making a promise you can keep.

Beyond those concerns, most book titles highlight a specific element of the story they're attached to, making this is a great place to start when titling your own novel. Here are some common naming conventions you might consider:

- **Character Names:** The Great Gatsby, Black Beauty
- **Descriptions:** The Hobbit, The Maze Runner
- **Locations or Settings:** Jurassic Park, Casablanca
- **Unique Objects or Elements:** The Maltese Falcon, The Golden Compass
- **An Important Event:** The Hunger Games, The Lord of the Rings: Return of the King
- **The Story's Core Idea:** How to Train Your Dragon, Star Wars

You may notice that a few of these are movie titles, but they follow the same basic principles as novels. In fact, movie titles can make great examples to look towards when titling your own novel, providing that much more material to inspire you!

Speaking of inspiration, if you're unsure which of these naming conventions would be a good fit for your novel, I encourage you to look up the current best sellers in your genre. Flip through the top twenty and write down any titles that catch your eye, and then consider what they have in common—do they all use a character's name, or do they focus on a core idea? Maybe they prefer objects or elements, or perhaps settings?

Regardless of which convention they use, you can take this information and apply it to your own novel. First, brainstorm a few keywords that represent your story. Then list one or two words for each of these groups, specifically choosing words that you think could fit in your title:

- Major characters
- Important events
- Key locations
- Unique objects
- Landmarks, creatures, or powers
- Adjectives that describe your story

From there, all you need to do is combine these words, using the example titles you picked out and the different naming conventions we looked at for inspiration. When doing so, remember to create a title that will spark interest in your reader—you want this title to draw them in and encourage them to keep reading, so lean on the most unique or intriguing aspects of your story. Think carefully about your target reader as well. Someone looking for a cozy romance novel probably wouldn't respond to a novel titled *The Killer's Daughter*, whereas a thriller reader might.

As you go through this process, read your work in progress titles out loud and listen to how they sound. The best novel titles have a rhythmic or even lyrical quality to them, not only making them easier to remember, but helping them stand out from the competition. If you can, try to achieve a similar effect for your own novel.

Finally, once you've chosen a title, do a quick online search. Is there another book, play, or movie with that exact title, or are there any similar to it? As frustrating as it is to realize someone else has already taken your dream title, you definitely don't want to copy a title from another story—not only will this make your novel harder to find for readers, but it's also bad practice.

Once you've found the right title for your story—one that isn't taken by another novel—write it at the top of your manuscript. Your novel is officially complete.

The Goals of Day Nine

You've walked a long road to get here but, as Day Nine comes to a close, your novel is finally ready. Your story is strong, your characters are compelling, and your prose is polished and proofread. However, today is only Day Nine—what about Day Ten?

Well, while this isn't the last day of this challenge, I won't spoil tomorrow's goals just yet. There's one final hurdle you'll have to overcome before your editing journey is truly complete, but until then, I hope you'll give yourself—and your eyes—a much-needed break. You've come so far over these last few weeks, and there isn't much further to go!

Tomorrow you'll face your final challenge, but for now, here are the goals you've completed for Day Nine:

1. Create a style guide for your novel that includes

names, usages, pronouns, and your story's tense.
2. Proofread your manuscript, checking for consistency, grammar, spelling, typos, and style.
3. Once your manuscript is proofread, finalize your novel's opening line.
4. Finish your novel by choosing a title.

On to Day Ten!

13

DAY TEN: THE SHIFT FROM AMATEUR TO AUTHOR

Over the years, I've heard many authors claim their characters talk to them, perhaps even taking control of their stories entirely. Personally, I think I'm a little too analytical to hear my character talking, but that doesn't mean I don't accept a fundamental truth—stories are living things. They'll grow and change in ways we never expected, eventually transforming into something all their own. That's both the beauty and the curse of being a writer—we aren't fully in control.

Unfortunately, with that fact comes a lot of anxiety. You no doubt started this adventure with a clear vision of the story you wanted to write and realizing that you failed to create that story can be downright painful. You want your novel to match that original idea even as your story evolves in another direction, and you're left wondering how other authors managed to breathe life into their "perfect" stories. How did *they* avoid this problem?

Well, in reality, this is a struggle nearly every author faces.

The stories we set out to write simply aren't the stories we end up creating, for a variety of reasons. That perfect idea we started with can't survive in the real world, and so we tweak and change it—and yes, even edit it—until it can finally stand on its own two legs. In the process, we lose something, but we also gain a lot. No writer escapes this reality, and no novel truly captures the idea that started it.

Still, accepting this is never easy. Perfectionism is a powerful beast, and many writers hold on to their novels forever, endlessly struggling to turn back the clock to that original vision. The more time passes, the more the story takes on a life of its own, branching out far beyond what that original idea could have ever captured. Unfortunately, many writers can't accept this and, as a result, their novels will never be truly complete.

In the end, this is the real difference between wanting to be an author and actually becoming one—authors know when to accept that their stories aren't their own.

One Final Reading

As we move into the final day of this challenge, your novel is officially in its final form, making this the perfect time to complete one final reading.

We've talked a lot about reading your novel aloud the last few days, and I've encouraged you to try it on multiple occasions. However, I know at least a few of you will have avoided doing so. Reading to yourself can be embarrassing, even with no one else around, but it's still an important part of experiencing your story. You've been staring at this manuscript for weeks now, and eventually the words on the page just stop meaning anything. Hearing them is the only way to gain a truly fresh perspective, so today I'm not giving you the option.

Your first goal for today is simple—read your story aloud and listen to how it sounds.

Just like on Day One, there are many ways to do this. Would printing your novel out help you focus, or would you prefer to read from a tablet or computer? Personally, the feeling of seeing my words on an e-reader is very validating, but you may get the same experience reading on paper—really, there's no right or wrong here. Some of you may even need your computer to read your manuscript to you, and that's ok too. Whatever the case may be, get your novel ready and settle it, because it's time to read it one final time.

As you read your story, there's no need for highlighters, pens, or pencils. For the most part, this is just about giving you one last moment with your story, a final send-off if you will. If you come across any lingering typos or errors, go ahead and fix them, but for the most part your novel should be in its final form. However, there are a few questions to keep in the back of your mind as you go:

- Did you keep your promises to your readers?
- Did you answer the questions you set up?
- Did your story's conflict reach a clear conclusion?
- Did each of your characters always have a goal pushing them forward?
- Did your internal logic stay consistent?
- Did you give your readers a satisfying payoff?
- Did your protagonist earn their victory or deserve their failure?
- Are you satisfied with the story you've created?

Even as you think about these questions, don't worry about them too much until you've finished reading your story. Instead, let them guide your thoughts as you experience the novel you've created. While your prose may not be perfect or your story may still have some flaws, if you can answer most of these questions with a confident "yes," then your editing journey is complete.

Becoming an Author

Though all the questions above are important in their own right, that last one is by far the most meaningful, so let me ask it again…

Are you satisfied with the story you've created?

At the end of the day, no novel is perfect. There will be flaws, both objective and subjective, and as the author you'll see those flaws more clearly than anyone else. You'll notice every scrap of stilted dialog, every poorly foreshadowed plot twist, and every incomplete character arc. You'll go back and read your novel a decade from now and catch a single typo in a panic, forced to wonder if every person who has ever read your story saw it too.

As hard as it is to accept, these flaws will never truly go away —every time you try to fix them, more will take their place, until eventually you have to accept your novel for what it is.

Unfortunately, this doesn't stop some writers from obsessing over their novels, and maybe you're feeling that way too. Perfectionism can cause some of this, but a lot of it could also be because of the realization that the story you've written isn't the story you set out to write.

You see, the more you keep writing, the more you'll evolve as a writer, and your ideas will evolve along with you. Not only that, but your skills and priorities will evolve too. On the one hand, when you discovered the original vision that would eventually become your novel, you likely placed all of your focus on a single scene, character, or idea. However, now you can see your novel as a larger whole. That scene will have changed, and the character you initially envisioned will have taken on a life of their own. While this is a beautiful process, it can still be difficult to accept the disconnect between where you started and where your novel has finished.

Ultimately, you have to embrace writing as an endless journey. For every new novel you write or story you read, you'll continue to learn and grow. This novel isn't the end of your writing life and, trust me—if you've gotten this far, you'll end up writing another one before too long. That should be an exciting thing, but to get there you have to accept that this novel doesn't need to be perfect. Perfection is nothing but a myth. Instead of chasing something you'll never find, strive to be proud of your writing both for the hurdles you've overcome and for the amazing story you've created, flaws and all.

If you can do that, then you're truly done with this challenge —not only is your novel complete, but you're ready to accept that completeness as well.

There are many next steps you could take from here, and all are equally valid. Maybe it's time to submit your novel to literary agents and publishing houses, or perhaps you'll turn your eyes towards self-publishing. Maybe this was only ever a personal project, one you're satisfied to have completed for its own sake, or perhaps you're already planning your authorial empire! Wherever you fall on this spectrum, it's up to you to decide what comes next.

In the end, the first step to becoming a successful author is knowing when to accept your novels for what they are. Every day you'll gain a new bit of writing skill, and your stories will never quite keep up. Yet, maybe that's a good thing—it's just one more reason to start working on your next creation as you wave this one off into the world.

Tomorrow you'll have officially created a finished novel, but for now, here are the goals you've completed for Day Ten:

1. Complete one final reading of your novel.
2. Prepare to send your novel out into the world— you've both earned it!

WHAT COMES NEXT?

As we reach the final moments of this challenge, I hope you're ready—you have an exciting future ahead of you!

Not only did you create a story and bring it to life out of nothing, but you've polished and refined it into a fully fledged novel. A lot of writers never reach this stage, so I hope you realize just how big of an accomplishment this is. While your journey isn't over just yet, you've made so much progress.

Of course, you may have questions about what comes next, in which case I encourage you to reach out and send me an email through my website!

When I'm not busy writing books like these and getting lost in my own fictional worlds, I run **The Novel Smithy**, a site dedicated to giving new writers the tools they need to create their dream novels.

Finally, if you enjoyed this book, leaving a review would not only help me, but other writers as well. Reviews are how readers like you find the books they're looking for, so I hope you'll take a moment to leave some honest feedback.

With that said, this book—and your editing challenge—is officially complete!

Happy writing,

Lewis

Before you go… **How well do you really know your hero?**

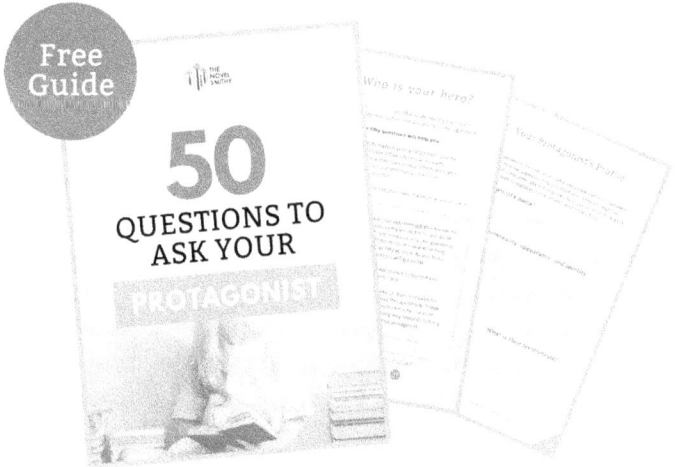

If you're ready to craft a vibrant, engaging protagonist, download your **FREE copy of 50 Questions to Ask Your Protagonist.**

This in-depth questionnaire is the perfect companion to this book, and the perfect way to get to know your hero!

https://thenovelsmithy.com/50-questions/

ABOUT THE AUTHOR

Lewis Jorstad is an editor and book coach who helps scrappy genre fiction authors (and soon-to-be authors) master their craft and find their readers. He's the bestselling author of seven guides for novelists, hosts a thriving community for storytellers inside The Forge, and runs one of The Write Life's 100 Best Websites for Writers.

When he isn't busy supporting students or writing books like this one, he spends far too much time watching squirrels from his office window in Central Virginia.

You can find more of his work over at **The Novel Smithy:**

https://thenovelsmithy.com/

"Books aren't written—they're rewritten. Including your own."

MICHAEL CRICHTON, AMERICAN NOVELIST AND
SCREENWRITER

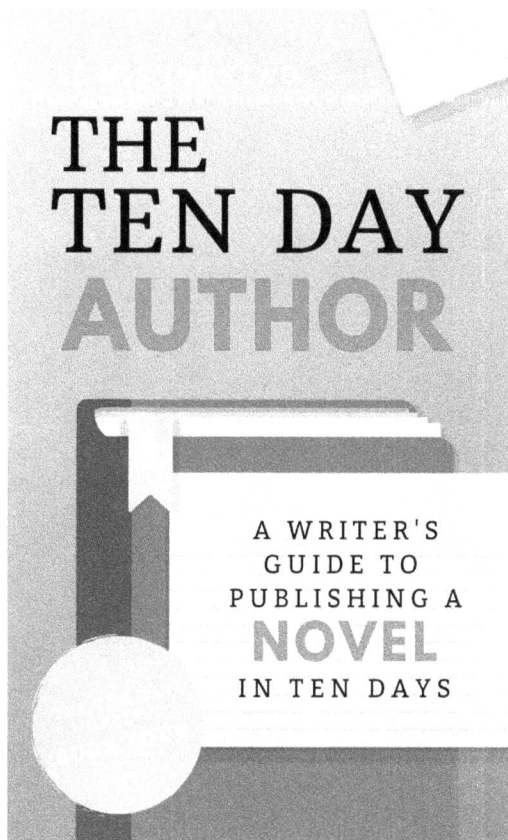

THE
TEN DAY
AUTHOR

A WRITER'S
GUIDE TO
PUBLISHING A
NOVEL
IN TEN DAYS

The day you become an author has arrived.

If you're ready to become a published author, check out the next
book in The Ten Day Novelist series: The Ten Day Author!

www.ingramcontent.com/pod-product-compliance
Lightning Source LLC
Chambersburg PA
CBHW060845280326
41934CB00007B/931